Apos

A
Kingdom Perspective
of the
Prophetic

"Kingdom Blessings,
"Elder Justice"

Apostle John Reed

Apostle John and LaTonya Reed Ministries
P.O. Box 500116
Atlanta, Ga. 31150

ISBN-10:1530980011
ISBN-13: 978-1530980017

To book Apostle John and/or Apostle LaTonya Reed for seminars, teachings, ministering, conferences, or book orders please contact them at the address above.

Dedications

To my lovely, adorable, beautiful, anointed, lovely Wife, Queen, best friend, Apostle, Prophetess, and Teacher LaTonya Reed – all of your wonderful support, patience, respect, commitment, dedication, prayers, fasting's, encouragement, words, and agape love has made me the man, and husband I am today. I so love and thank God for you because you are my wife for life!

To my wonderful parents Deacon John A. Reed and Florine Reed for being Godly parents and showing me the love that the Bible declares parents should show. They brought me up in the ways of the Lord and have always encouraged me. They birthed who God planned! They are the greatest parents on earth!

To Pastor and Prophet Raymond Jones who has always been a very needed and strong prophetic voice in my life from a teenager on, as well as a spiritual Father in the gospel.

To Prophet Jean M. Domoraud, another spiritual Father in my life who speaks accurate prophetic words and although he is very busy in ministry travels, he always makes time.

To the most humble Bishop I know, Bishop Brandon B. Porter. He is a true inspiration and genius in ministry, who is always about the work of the Kingdom of God.

To all the readers and students of the Word of God and prophecy, may this Kingdom book enlarge your knowledge and revelation of the communication of the Lord. May it help build from where you are and take you into deeper dimensions in the realm of the voice of the Lord in your endeavors with the Lord.

To the one and only source of all Knowledge, Wisdom, Love, the Creator, my Sustainer, my King, my Lord, my Rock, my All and All. I am so blessed to be in the Kingdom of God! To God be all the Glory, Honor, and Praise!

Introduction

This book was prophetically birthed, written and designed in order to address the Lords prophetic communication in many ways from a Kingdom perspective since God is a King.

The best information to receive is always from the originating source. Ignorance has for the longest become such an attacker, that the result of destruction is actually birthed as a result and from ignorance and whatever we ignore we become ignorant of.

Our King and Lord does not want us to be ignorant of his gifts and so we must gain complete truth and correct knowledge of the Royal Word of God, which I call the Royal Constitution of Heaven, to stand against the confusing darkness of religion, wrong traditions, and man-made theological assumptions and hypotheses.

The way to combat all the many misconceptions of truth is to extrapolate from the Constitution of Heaven and see what the mind of the King is concerning various subject matters. There is so much there is to know concerning the prophetic that the church does not understand, and therefore what we do not understand we barely engage in which causes us to miss out on so much that the Lord has to offer and give to us.

As you read this book, pray that the Lord will give you an open mind to receive, understand, and then to engage in the beautiful awesome realm of the prophetic. Although there is so much we can cover because the prophetic is so exhaustive, we pray that we enlighten you to a very great portion for your understanding, enrichment, and move in what God is saying to you, the nation, the world, and his Kingdom!

Contents

Chapter 1

The Cause of Prophetic Misunderstandings

Many times when I am doing a seminar, a conference, or just teaching the gospel of the Kingdom of God, I always have the people listening say "Lord damage my ignorance!" The reason is because this book, and many teachings I teach are birthed out of ignorance. What do you mean Apostle?

Ignorance is actually having a lack of knowledge in an area, but it is repaired by knowledge, and light against darkness. So therefore ignorance in any area causes defeat in that area, and this is why knowledge must be given in the area of ignorance, and so ignorance has actually caused truth to bring in liberty and understanding, instead of darkness and defeat.

When the Word of God speaks of darkness, in many cases it is representative of ignorance, and light is usually representative of knowledge and the church in many cases has really done an excellent job in teaching errors! These errors have caused so much frustration in the body that discouragement becomes inevitable, division becomes obvious, disagreement is birthed, and separation is clear.

It is very hard to engage in that which we do not understand. For instance, one of the reasons why so many ministries have poor attendance at prayer meetings is because many do not understand prayer, and because of that, discouragement again is now inevitable. Besides, prayer is not a religious activity; it is actually a legal Kingdom activity. Oh Lord, this will get me in trouble; we will save that for another book. So destruction is the result of ignorance, and ignorance is dark bondage with what you do not understand.

In Hosea 6:4, it quotes something amazing to me that most preachers do not fully quote. We quote a small portion of it. In Hosea 4:6 says *"My people are destroyed for lack of knowledge...."*

The word "destroyed" here in the Hebrew means to be cut off, caused to cease, and/or to perish. However there is more to this verse than we thought or than we quote. It continues by saying *"because thou hast rejected knowledge, I will also reject thee, that thou shalt be no priest to me: seeing thou hast forgotten the law of thy God, I will also forget thy children."*

Do you see how deep this actually is? He is saying knowledge was available, because you cannot reject that which was not available. The Kings people here are rejecting knowledge that is available, and perishing because of rejecting knowledge.

He is not done, he continues by letting us know he will reject YOU. Why? It is because if you are ignorant, then you cannot represent him, you cannot even be a priest to him, and since you forgot the law, I will forget your children too. It is because you will teach your children and the next generation the same thing, error, and ignorance, along with tradition that may not be of the Word of the Lord.

Can I tell you what actually makes the Word of God have no effect? Mark 7:13 says *"Making the word of God of non-effect through **your tradition,** which ye have delivered: and many such like things do ye."*

"We have been so Religionized instead of Kingdomized!"

There are so many who are so baptized in certain traditions to the point that even if they read a scripture in the Bible itself, if tradition does not agree, then neither will they. Since when have we allowed tradition and religion to trump the Word?

Religion does not care about people being saved, the Kingdom does! This is why there are different religions of practice. This is all so important to understanding why there are so many misunderstandings of the prophetic, but I am only stretching this subject just to give you an even broader understanding of the widespread cause of ignorance in the body of Christ.

First, Jesus never brought a religion; he restored and brought the Kingdom. Religion is full of rituals. The only thing Jesus ever preached on earth was the gospel of the Kingdom of God, he never preached opinions! This is why in Matthew 4:17, it mentions the first public statement of Jesus which was repent, change your mind, and thinking.

"We have been so heavily Religionized instead of Kingdomized."

We have been so imbued with religion that we believe religion even over the Word of God. When I say we are religionized, I am saying we have been baptized and submerged in so many rituals, beliefs, as well as so much bondage that we don't even understand what the Kingdom of God is about, and again that is all Jesus taught and preached.

When I use the word Kingdomized, it came out of me when I was ministering about the Kingdom of God and religion once. When I use the word Kingdomized, it has a broad meaning, but I will simply shorten it here. To be "Kingdomized" is to be fully submerged into the Kings ideas, government, culture, ways, principles, and of course the King himself. That is being in the Kingdom of God, and that is part of what the Kingdom is about. It is about dominion, it is understanding the ways of the Constitution of Heaven, the Bible, which is the Word of God. As we are walking in this ascended lifestyle of Kingdom standards, it is then and at that time that we are also starting to walk in Kingdomization!

"Darkness and religion is like amniotic fluid in which ignorance can flourish"

Many prophetic misunderstandings are due to the ignorance of the Word, bad traditions, and religious misunderstandings.

Just because a person grows older, it does not mean they are necessarily more knowledgeable. A lot of times it just makes the present ignorance more mature. So we have to peel off the old stamped on ignorance with the revelatory true knowledge from the Royal Constitution of Heaven.

Religion has caused many wars, disruption of churches, deceit against liberty and freedom in the Holy Spirit, as well as chaos against divine scripture. There are many in the Church today that don't even believe that there are Prophets, less Apostles, due to ignorance and religion.

This is why I can say for a fact prophetically that the Kingdom manifestations of the multiple many displays of the King are really going to mess people's minds up when they see it. The Lord revealed one time to me that he does not need nobody to defend him concerning the things he is about to do through people who are hungry for the Lord, right in front of those who do not even believe.

In the sections of the Word of God in Mathew, Luke and Mark we read of their accounts at the time when Jesus was on the mountain and his clothing glistened with his radiant Glory.

They witnessed the last message coming to an end, and the fulfilment of another one, the gospel of the Kingdom of God. Now when they looked up, the only one left was Jesus and the voice of God saying hear ye HIM. Not the Prophets speaking he is coming, but HIM speaking HE is here with the message of the Kingdom of God.

Peter had the voice of the religious church today, the religious church wants to still keep that which the Lord God has let go and furthermore build a house for it. In this case three. This is what religion wants, it wants to build a house and freeze the dead! Darkness and religion is like the amniotic fluid in which ignorance can flourish.

Religion is really man's program, along with man's ways. The average religious Christian knows very little about the gospel of the Kingdom of God, and therefore does not come to grip with subjects that are from a Kingdom perspective, and the prophetic is one.

Many people think the prophetic is pathetic, or not real, but it is real and we will get into the understanding of the prophetic from a Kingdom perspective.

In John the 8th chapter and the 12th verse, Jesus indicates that he is the Light of the world. Metaphorically speaking, he is saying that he is bringing us knowledge to the world. If we follow in his knowledge we will not stumble in ignorance! Therefore the enemy will always rule to the measuring degree of your ignorance! We supply him that portion of dominion over our lives and therefore the good news of truth is hid in darkness.

Religion has hijacked the fundamentals of truth! Jesus never brought a religion; he brought a government on his shoulders per Isaiah 9:6, 7. Religious people have attacked the voice of God, the Word of God, the prophetic and all that comes with it. Religion attacks the Kingdom of God. They came against prayers in school, and then the ten commandment slabs at different places, and much more because you can stop religion. Why follow religion when it does not last? You can stop religion, but can you stop American citizenship? No you cannot stop it.

American citizenship is not something you do so you cannot stop it, but religion is something you do. You cannot stop me from being my Fathers son, but you can fire a servant. We are citizens of the Kingdom of God and must understand our rights, and we have governmental rights in the Kingdom of God, and one of those rights is to know the truth!

Religion actually replaces the truth with traditions! Jesus had issues with all the religious folk because remember they knew everything. We don't want to just educate your head but to activate your spirit, and religion tries to suffocate, smother and kill your spirit so that you will not receive the prophetic understanding of the Lord.

We have been so heavily educated with the contamination of truth to the point that when the truth comes, we fight against it. We must understand that the enemy of the Kingdom of God is really ignorance and that ignorance has now caused so many misunderstandings.

"Good deliveries with wrong information, causes successful contamination!"

This is why the Word tells us to study, to show ourselves approved, rightly dividing the Word of truth. When we study we are doing a detailed investigation and analysis on a given particular subject. Studying takes time and effort. We must also pray for clarity because good deliveries with wrong information, causes successful contamination.

You were not born to live in the kingdom of darkness and this is why Jesus told Nicodemus you must be born again. So in our born again state we must be filled with the knowledge of the truth concerning the prophetic, and everything else in the Constitution of Heaven.

Tradition has become such an upset against the church when it comes down to really understanding the prophetic. Many were raised under a certain denomination, or belief that they did not do this or that when they were growing up. Some people have even used the term "I caught the Holy Ghost."

Anyway, traditions have been here for the longest. Traditions exist in every single nation, culture, and generation. Tradition has furnished many with their identity, so pure tradition is good. Notice, I said pure tradition is good.

I believe that one reason the church cannot reach the world is because of bad tradition. As a matter of fact, the church can barely reach itself due to bad tradition or tradition that is not in pure form.

Tradition is the inherited handing down of different beliefs, customs, ideas and many cultural ways of doing things from generation to generation. It is an established inherited way of thinking and or acting. According to what traditional values a person has, can easily determine if they believe in the move of the prophetic, Prophets, lifting hands, speaking in tongues, dancing unto the Lord, singing, clapping, praising, lifting your voice and other forms of praise etc. The list really goes on.

Coming up in service, I remember as a youth, a youth leader telling me while I was snapping my fingers to gospel music that the snapping of the fingers was a sin and I should stop. I asked how and why it was a sin to snap my fingers. The youth leader stated that it was worldly. Of course I asked how the snapping of my fingers was considered a worldly thing. Well, the reply was that people in the world do it and so we are not supposed to do it. This reply was clearly based on traditional beliefs.

Now look at the definition of snapping your finger and let us examine if this is a sin. To snap your finger means to make a noise by pushing one finger hard against your thumb! I believe the Bible tells me to make a joyful noise. Why would that style of noise be a sin? I can clap, but not snap? As a musician, I know some of us snap our fingers to keep the rhythm.

It did not destroy me because I knew better from the Word of God, thank God. However I was often attacked with certain drum beats that was considered worldly as well. I asked if they knew what the lust of the world was. Apparently what I was doing was it. My point is that we have taken things too far to the point where it causes unnecessary hindrance to the freedom of praise to the Lord, and to being receptive to things the Lord actually enjoys.

I was told dancing is also a sin due to traditions. Now if I can dance for the Lord, then dancing in itself for the Lord is not a sin. Either dancing is a sin, or it is not. Again my point is we take some things too far. The bible encourages us to dance for the Lord.

So when you look at the definition of tradition you can see the problem. It is inherited thinking, not Kingdom repentance.

I heard a story told different ways, but to make the point I will share it. A girl would cut the sides of her ham, and throw it away. Others being concerned would ask why she cut off all that good ham. She would reply by indicating that she never asked her mother why, her mother did it and it was a family tradition. In turn her mother would reply that her mother did it. So finally when the inquisitors called the mothers mother and asked about the reason of cutting the ham, she indicated the pan was not big enough to hold the ham back then.

See wrong tradition cuts away and destroys. This is why I do not ever preach sermons because a sermon is actually just a religious dissertation. I do not preach religion, I preach what Jesus preached, the great gospel of the Kingdom of God. If we would teach the truth it would cut down a lot of confusion, so since God is not the author of confusion. It makes you wonder who is anointing people to confuse us in the preaching of error.

So we can easily see that religion, tradition, and ignorance of not knowing the truth of the Word of God creeps up against understanding the prophetic. When I am invited to a ministry to minister, I make sure they understand that I move in the gifts of the spirit, and if there is an issue with that, let me know beforehand.

The good thing is that when they invite me you would have to have known that already anyway. So many in the church have downplayed the prophetic. They just do not believe that God speaks anymore, or speaks at all. The Lord wants to speak in so many ways which we will get into, but leaders are against it because of ignorance, religion, and traditional ways.

"I prophesy that God is touching hearts and we shall see the display of the prophetic like never before and God will back it up with Kingdom demonstrations in a way that we have never witnessed."

The prophetic is so very misunderstood to the point that it cannot progress forward and be a blessing to the church at large without battles. People that come against the prophetic block the flow of the Holy Spirit in more ways than they can imagine. The Bible declares to quench not the Holy Spirit.

We should allow the Holy Spirit to flow as he wills and as he wants as we move in order with him

The word quench here should be brought out so to give you more clarity in understanding. In 1 Thessalonians 5:19, it tells us clearly that we should not quench the Holy Spirit. When we say quench, it actually means to extinguish. Extinguishers are used to put out fires. Hebrews 12:29 tells us that our God is a consuming fire, so why do we put God out?

Traditions are designed to capture or preserve an experience, truth, or fact. It is a means to an end, and a means comes to an end. When tradition replaces truth, and becomes that truth, it then must be destroyed or quenched.

The ham was too big for the pan, because they did not have a pan big enough, but three generations later that was not true anymore! The girl never asked her mother why she threw away all the sides of the ham, because a generation who asks why, is called rebellious by the generation that does not even know why. Most of the times, the answers to the questions of why, is the answer that says, this is how we always did it. So tradition can become the graveyard of a cemetery reality if we are not careful.

Tradition is a servant of truth but not always truth. Again, the goal of tradition is to preserve, protect and deliver the actual experience of truth, but that is not always the case. Tradition is only as valuable as the original truth it was supposed to relay.

"Tradition can become the graveyard of a cemetery reality."

One of the enemies that attempts to trump knowledge is tradition, so we must be careful that we do not allow it to step upon truth.

"Tradition does not always mean that the one alive is living, but the one that's dead is alive!"

10

We have to stop waking up the part of tradition that has no fact of truth to become alive when it should be dead. Tradition does not always mean that the one alive is living, but the one that's dead is alive. In other words, folk who are alive on dead tradition, is bringing the dead tradition back to life.

I have been to a ministry where the women sit on the left, and the men sit on the right, but at home they sleep in the same bed! That is tradition.

I have seen some folk say that if you call on Jesus name real fast that is speaking in tongues because they exclaim that traditionally fast talking was tongues.

So the list goes on, and the prophetic is suffering because people are saying that God does not move that way anymore.

I will say that the prophetic has been damaged due to people allowing the flesh to get into the way and deliver what they want to say, instead of what God actually said. One of the greatest causes and dangers to the prophetic is when you mix what you desire the hearer to hear, verses what God desires the hearer to hear. So there can be a misunderstanding in the prophetic based on what you thought you heard, verses what was really said.

Let me hurry and get back to the points of truth I have already made in reference to letting go of traditional things that may not be truthful things. Here is food for thought. If you used an instrument for triumphant victory at one time in your life, you would probably want to use it again; however that may not always be the best thing to use for the next victory.

That seems as though that makes no sense if it was helpful and victorious for you in the past right? Well let me show you something.

I want to explain a scriptural truth to you. In Judges 15, God anointed a bone for a particular assignment to be used by Samson to kill a thousand men. Samson never used it again. It was for that time, and he never went back to use it again, he threw away success!

Many things that worked then may not work now, we are under a better covenant! So we cannot allow what we may have been handed down from experience or tradition, or denomination, or religion, to suffocate the prophetic move of the Lord.

There are many reasons for misunderstanding prophecies but the cause still trumps as ignorance. There is for example what is called or classified as "conditional prophecies" that we see in the Word. If we believe every prophetic word uttered will come to pass, then we have indicated that we did not understand conditional prophecies.

A conditional prophecy is a prophetic word that does not happen unless conditions apply to it. Nineveh for instance would have been destroyed but there was a condition. This is just a little example of what I am saying, but it is things like this that causes misunderstandings of the prophetic, however it is still due to ignorance.

The Word of God declares in 2 Corinthians 2:11 that we are not ignorant concerning satans devices lest he take advantage over us. In other words ignorance of his schemes will cause him to have an advantage over us. Here we see the damage of ignorance again according to the Word.

Ephesians 4:18 indicates to us that when our understanding is darkened it alienates us from the life of God, due to the blindness of our hearts.

These scriptures are pretty much explaining what ignorance causes. So again I cannot stress enough how important it is for us to understand that the attack of ignorance, and the laziness to study the Word of God causes a misunderstanding of the prophetic.

"Truth should never be stuck in the middle, it should always be right and untruth left!"

It is amazing how the truth must always fight and yet it always takes a stand. Many come against the prophetic moves of God, and the truth of God, allowing things that are not true to swallow up truth.

We must get past doctrinal issues and presentations of attacks against the truth. Truth is from the original source, the Word of God is truth. John 8:32 plainly tells us that we shall know the truth and the truth shall make us free.

Sad to say, but many in the church world do not even quote this truthfully; they say it shall "set you free." See the problem we have with truth?

We even declare so many scriptures that are not even in the Word of God due to our own application of scripture, and we carry it for centuries. Here is a famous one, "try the spirit by the spirit." Where is that scripture found? Read what 1 John 4:1 says. The bible does not even say "spare the rod, spoil the child", what it actually says can be read it in Proverbs 13:24.

I can go on for a while and list quite a few, like we say there is a mansion in the sky, but so you will not be disappointed, the word mansion in the Word there in John means .....places, and places are rooms, in his Father's house, not houses.

So when looking at truth, truth should never be stuck in the middle; it should always be right and untruth left. Never be in the balance of the in-between, be on the weight of truth. I like how 2 Peter 1:12 tells us to be established on the present truth.

We have gotten away from the truth which is another cause for the misunderstanding of the prophetic. Paul the Apostle of Jesus Christ asked who bewitched you oh foolish Galatians that you should not obey the truth? This is still the question we need to ask today and the answer is what I am explaining, ignorance, tradition, religion, and such alike.

It seems in every evolution of ministry there is the biblically uneducated that will never come into the truth, and that is the truth. If we would live by every word that proceeded out of the mouth of God, we would not stop at the bread of man!

Tradition, religion, ignorance, and the like will always put the characters of yesterday against the awesome mighty move of God today. Religion says man's way to appease and to please God is the way, not what the Bible says, but what man says.

I have discovered over the years that the misrepresentation by the applied misinterpretation of scripture is a strong cause of misunderstanding the prophetic because if you do not apply the principles of interpretation, you will not understand the meaning. One thing is for sure, and that is that we cannot read an eastern book with a western mind!

The Bible as we know was written in Hebrew, some Aramaic, and Greek. So we must understand the correct translation of a word to get the correct and full meaning. You cannot apply our western culture with and eastern culture and get the same meaning, it just won't work.

Many people also think prophecy is foretelling the future due to not understanding, and we will get into this explanation in Chapter 3 of this book later on. However we apply definitions that may not even go with our modern understanding. This can cause problems with the entire Word of God for sure in our understanding if we are not careful to rightly divide the Word of truth.

So if we are not taught the truth about the prophetic, then we will always continually walk into the darkness concerning it, and then we will never allow it to bring to light the revelation it is purposed to fulfil.

God wants to deposit his perspective in our minds and hearts, concerning the prophetic and all else that concerns the Lord. To see beyond where you are at, stop finishing where you are.

We must move in a time where we are picking up the frequencies of heaven to cause a distortion to channels that are not programmed by God! Read Proverbs 2:1-5.

Chapter 2

The Cure for Prophetic Misunderstandings

We have now discussed quite a few causes of many prophetic misunderstandings and the great thing is that the Constitution of Heaven gives us the cure. There is a cure against tradition that is not pure or not of the Word, religions that tie and place us in bondage, misinterpretation of scripture and even fear and rejection of the prophetic and so much more that causes misunderstandings of the prophetic.

Whenever there is a problem, God has a solution. Knowledge and information causes a transformation.

One cure for prophetic misunderstandings is the revelation of truth revealed, however we must understand what it is about the truth that shall truly make us free. So, let us go back to a scripture in the Constitution of Heaven, the Bible, and the Word of God. In John the 8th chapter verses 31 and 32, it says something we often miss out on. It says *"Then said Jesus to those Jews which believed on him, If ye continue in my word, then are ye my disciples indeed; And you shall know the truth, and the truth shall make you free."*

"You are as free as the truth you know!"

Notice you shall know the truth. Now the word "know" in the Greek here is *ginosko*, which means to understand. The knowledge of truth is one thing, but knowing it is another. So the condition of the truth that shall make you free is knowing it. Therefore the amount of truth you know will determine the amount of freedom you will experience. So you are as free as the truth you know, and to add more, you are also as bound in what you don't know.

So if we continue in his Word, and not the bread of man, but the bread of life that has no expiration date, we will see that it is full of life!

Look at verse 36 in the same chapter of John 8; it says if the Son therefore shall make you free, ye shall be free indeed! He is saying if you get the information from me, the original source, then you got the original truth! If you get a computer and do not read the manual you will only enjoy the part you know, but as you abide in the manual, you will know so much more and therefore experience more than you knew.

Knowing truth cancels out the foreknowledge and operational old experience that may not be full truth.

I must say a very powerful statement that we will place in the center in bold so that it stands out to you, the reader, when it comes to experience.

"Experience is NOT the best Teacher, but Evaluated Experience is!"

Never ever lower the standards of your expectations or of the scriptures with the past levels of your experience. I must say experience is not the best teacher because your experience can cause you to be stuck in your past and then freeze you at that moment if you allow it to.

This is the reason that ongoing training is needed by doctors to keep them informed of different sicknesses, diseases, new medicines, and operational procedures. Continuous training prevents the lack of more knowledge being attained because out of all you know, there is still more to know.

For top performance, if experience was enough, then more training would never be necessary.

So experience is not the best teacher but I would say evaluated experience is. If you only hang out with that which could have been, then you will lose excitement of what could be. One of the greatest enemy threats of moving ahead is the excitement of where you are.

The manufacturer is the only one that knows and understands its invention and product, so why go along with everyone else that only guesses and supposes? This is why your knowledge should come from the manufacturer and not the retailer because the retailer is in it for the sales only. Manuals are not authored and produced by customers, so do not let them tell you how it works!

A manual is a makers mind placed on paper and he wants you to read his mind about what he produced so you can know the truth and so the truth can make you free!

So one of the greatest cures for prophetic misunderstanding is knowing the truth from the manual of the King which is none other than his Word.

I must repeat, God is King! In Psalm 24:7-8, he is called the King of Glory and a King is a ruler. A King has a Kingdom and a Kingdom is a Kings Domain or territory and a King is a ruler over his territorial domain. It is a must that we readjust our pattern of thinking, repent and have our minds and our lives baptized into the Kingdom of God. To repent means to change your mind, and thinking. When our thinking becomes Kingdomized so will our actions and understanding.

If we would begin to think like the King, our actions would be kingly, and we can bring his thoughts into the worlds systems here on earth. Imagine bringing his perspective to all of man's problems and man returning back to the King! Oh my, oh my oh my!

The King always wanted to establish his Kingdom on earth, so in Genesis 1:26, he clearly said let us make man in our image and likeness and let them have dominion, wow! Dominion is the Hebrew word "radah", the Greek word "basileia" and it's the Aramaic word "mamlaka" and they all mean and refer to dominion, rulership, royal power and government.

So then a Kingdom is the realm in which the King rules and transfers his will to those who belong to him. So the cure for prophetic misunderstandings comes from knowing what the King is saying about his origination of prophecy in the first place. Original truth from the King is in his Constitution.

Now then, what is a constitution? A constitution is a body of fundamental principles that a country is governed by. God is the King of the Kingdom of Heaven and please take note that Heaven does have a structure and that is because Heaven is a country and a country is a nation that has its own government occupying a particular territory and Heaven is a territory.

Now then, what is a government? Government is the power to enforce its laws in a particular territory. The first government that ever existed is the Kingdom or Government of Heaven.

So in Genesis 1:26, God gave man governmental rule over the earth to represent the government of heaven. So we are in the Kingdom of God.

This is a sensitive subject for me and so dear to my heart when it comes to the Lords Kingdom so therefore another book will be forthcoming concerning the Kingdom of God.

I have been ministering about the Kingdom since 1987 because it is all Jesus preached and the whole Constitution of Heaven is not a religious book, but a Kings Manual, it is about a King, his Kingdom, and his Royal family.

So we must know about the Constitution of Heaven because it will bring truth and we must know truth concerning the Kings thoughts on the prophetic and everything else, but just to stay on the subject we are referring to the prophetic.

Every government has a constitution and as previously stated the Bible is the Royal Constitution of Heavens government. We are royal regents and a royal regent is a person appointed to administer for royalty and God is our Royal King, so we want to show you the cure for misunderstanding the prophetic and that is in his Constitution.

So, what then is a constitution? Simply put, a constitution is a body of fundamental principles to which a state or organized political community is to be governed. The constitution of the Royal Nation of God contains, like other constitutions, rights of citizens, laws, and the Bible contains just that.

So we will refer to the Word of God at times going forward as the Royal Constitution or the Constitution of Heaven for our Kingdom understanding.

To help you along the way this is how we will refer to the Word here to get your mind Kingdomized.

Article – The Book
Section – The Chapter
SubSection – The Verse

Paul said in Article 1 Corinthians Section 12 Subsection 1 (for the religious – 1 Corinthians 12:1) that he would not have us ignorant concerning the gifts of the Spirit. So we want to know the Kingdom perspective of the prophetic through the Royal Constitution of Heaven. If we know the Kings intellect on the prophetic we should be able to drop ours and obtain his. This is the cure, the Lord's Word.

Chapter 3

The Defining of the Prophetic

The prophetic is a wonderful part of the Kings expression, for without it, we would surely be void of knowing him, knowing his will, his desires, his purposes for us, his instructions, his laws, or his paths for us.

We would be void of getting a grasp even of his existence, his love, his gifts, his government, his provisions, his Fathering Spirit, his concern, and his care.

We would also be void of his rulership, his intents, his mind, his Mighty Kingdom, his compassion, his teachings, his laws, his word, his structure, his glory, his power, his omnipotence, his greatness, his faithfulness, his character, his attributes, his wisdom, his knowledge, and his understanding.

We would also be void of his great awesomeness and might, his peace that he gives, and so much more if it were not for the prophetic.

How would we live without his voice? How would we live without his words? For man cannot live by bread alone but by every word that proceedeth out of the mouth of God. His words are life and Spirit!

There are never any expiration dates to the prophetic, it would be totally impossible to ever have an expiration date to the prophetic, not even in eternity because the prophetic is the communication of God the King and Lord himself, and he will never stop communicating and therefore the prophetic will never end.

The King has countless ways of communication and we never want to box it up one way or another. Not one snowflake is alike, so that alone should tell us that the King has numerous ways of relating to us prophetically. In chapter 6 we will indulge you with some of the many ways the prophetic is displayed.

The prophetic is the Lord and King revealing himself to us. The prophetic reveals the very existence of the Lord our King. The prophetic released all that was created through his words.

"The prophetic is the inner release of God to the outer receivers of God!"

Everything that God pours out of himself is poured into the receiver, and God created everything, man has only put what God already created together to invent certain things, but God is creator. So the prophetic is the inner release of God to the outer receivers of God.

When we block and come against the prophetic move of the Lord, we then block the prophetic, because the prophetic is the outpouring of the Lord, for the testimony of Jesus Christ is the Spirit of prophecy.

The prophetic portrays the very presence of God in relaying something he wants to share with us. Prophecy is the flow of what the King wants to impart. Prophecy emanates from divine inspiration declaring what the Lord is saying.

Therefore preaching under the divine inspiration of the Holy Spirit is a form of prophecy but not its limit. One of the main purposes of the prophetic ministry is to bring us to a maturity, through the exposed will of the King.

The Lord told me that prophecy is the flowing of rivers out of the belly of his Spirit! Wow! This tells me that our spirit should never be a lake because lakes do not flow.

The Royal Constitution says in Article John Section 7 Subsection 38, that out of our bellies shall flow rivers of living water. The prophetic flow from the Lord through us should become streams into those who are thirsty for the prophetic voice of the Lord.

The prophetic can speak from what has not become, into what has been and reveal what will yet be. The prophetic is so important and needed in the Kingdom today. Ok, I am getting ahead of myself; let us go back into more of the expository of the definitions of the prophetic.

In defining the prophetic, it is very important to understand that there are different definitions of some prophetic words.

For a clear explanation, the word prophecy in the Greek is the word profeteiah and it is divine spoken communication. The word prophesy is the Hebrew word naba, which is to speak under the influence of the Spirit of God.

The prophetic in itself is not who you are going to marry, and you are going to get a house, and you are going to be wealthy, the prophetic is the voice of God that comes to edify, exhort, and comfort, and so much more. Not that those words are not comforting, but the simple prophetic explanation is clear in scripture again to edify, exhort and comfort.

Prophecy in the New Testament is forth-telling, not for-telling. Forth-telling usually refers to speaking of futuristic things, but simple for-telling is that word that is coming forth. We will get more into this as we go along but it is important to understand that and the concepts of the prophetic.

Prophecy reveals the thoughts of God. The prophetic and the office of the Prophet is also the extension of the ministry of Jesus the Christ.

I know I am supposed to reserve the ways of the prophetic for another chapter but in explaining the definition of the prophetic, I am compelled by the Spirit of the Lord to get this word in your hearing and spirit. So I will say something and that is we must understand that the Prophetic Word of God is not always sent to be heard! I am still defining with a stretch here.

In Article Psalm Section 107 Subsection 20, it says he sent his word and healed them. A word to heal is not always a word to hear!

"The prophetic word of God is not always sent to be heard!"

The prophetic word can also be defined in the category of manifestation. The centurion said just speak the word and my servant shall be healed, in other words he said send your mouth to my house.

The word can be sent by an errand to manifest and not to be heard. A go word to be sent to heal and not be heard! The prophetic brings manifestation! I have sent and spoke words under the Holy Spirit that were never heard in the ears, but healed in body parts! If you keep focusing on hearing you may miss your healing!

I prophesy that there are going to be prophetic healings entering the body to the person that never heard! This is the side of the prophetic we must adhere to and not box in. He that hath an ear let him hear what the Spirit says to the Church, so everyone does not have ears, so thank God the word can pass the ear and manifest with just an assignment!

The servant never heard anything, he only experienced the manifestation! When God speaks a word, do not pay attention to just what you hear, pay attention to what is manifested.

In Article Genesis Section 15 Subsection 1, the word of the Lord came to Abram in a vision. His words never return unto him void because however it comes it must accomplish the reason the Lord sent it. The vision was heard!

In The Royal Constitution, it mentions in Article Luke Section 4 Subsection 32, that they were astonished because his words were with authority or in other words with power. So apart from what he said, something had to happen after he spoke!

Everyone may not have the ears to hear but everything created does. Jesus spoke to the winds and commanded them to be at peace. He spoke to the winds and seas and the winds and seas obeyed him. The word peace that he spoke actually means to muzzle your mouth! He wanted the storms mouth muzzled because the storm was speaking back indicating by its actions that it wanted to take them out, and kill them. Your bills speak too, if they are not paid, you will hear them say we are shutting off.

This is the reason why that he was able to speak to the fig tree because it heard, and his words manifested results! So the prophetic is also in manifestation. Things manifest when the prophetic goes forth. When God speaks there must be a manifestation of that truth.

I remember in a service I had asked if anyone had a leg shorter than the other and I indicated before I prayed that the leg will grow out, and it did, but I spoke the manifestation will surely happen because when you speak it under the divine anointing and inspiration of the Spirit of the Lord, you do not have to wait for the manifestation.

We did not pray it will grow out, we spoke it would! I have seen so many miracles as a result of the spoken word of God that it excites me as I think and write about it.

So there is a lot concerning the prophetic and the defining of it, but again it is so exhaustive that in this book we just want to cover enough to launch you into a better understanding from the King's perspective.

I believe it is very important here to explain a little about the anointing. We do hear about it in the prophetic but what is the anointing, or a prophetic anointing?

The anointing is a supernatural application or enablement of power, and authority upon and in an individual to carry out a task or assignment for God. Likewise, the prophetic anointing is the supernatural application or enablement of power and authority upon an individual to carry out the prophetic for God.

In Article Acts Section 28 Subsection 32 it reads *"How God anointed Jesus of Nazareth with the Holy Ghost and with power: who went about doing good, and healing all that were oppressed of the devil; for God was with him."*

So here we read how God anointed, enabled, empowered, and placed a supernatural endowment of power on Jesus and he went about healing all that were oppressed of the devil for God was with him. The anointing is that power from God to deliver from oppression, to make free, to destroy yokes, etc.

So with the prophetic anointing, God engages his children to move, speak and flow in the prophetic. The anointing to move prophetically can come on an animal to even prophesy. If you did not know that, you can ask Balaam's ass.

In Article Numbers Section 22 Subsection 28, you can read that his ass spoke to him as she saw the angel of the Lord. The anointing works as God wills it to work and the anointing will find you when people around you will not even notice you.

You remember when David was in the back with the sheep and the Prophet Samuel was sent to anoint one of Jesses sons?

In Article 1 Samuel, you can read the story, it is exciting and yet there are so many truths to it as well. The Lord tells the Prophet Samuel to go past his mourning concerning Saul, and fill the horn with oil and then go to Jesse's house because God wanted to anoint one of Jesses sons as his king.

Notice before he could go, he took an anointing (oil). Notice how the people trembled at the coming of the Prophet because they did not know what word he will bring. They recognized this Prophet spoke what God said, period.

The Prophet saw one son and figured by looks that this was the one, but the Lord told him it was not and to not look on the outward appearance. After Jesse had his sons pass by the Prophet, notice how that the Prophet did not count against what the Lord told him. He could have figured that he missed it or the Lord missed it because he did not see any more sons, but he held on to the word of the Lord despite how it seemed and looked.

He could have said well ok, maybe I was just wrong and just thought God said what I thought he said. Then he asked if this was all of them. Now notice this, when you read the story, Jesse was calling them all by their names, but in referring to the youngest that was working, tending to the sheep, he never even called his name at all, and it obviously seemed as though he was not even invited to the sacrifice with the rest.

Sometimes due to your age, or being in the back, or not being noticed by family or just being left out, attracts the anointing. Can any good thing come out of Nazareth?

Notice that little David was working! He had a concerned heart, for he did the job of a servant and yet as a shepherd tending sheep. He had fought the lion behind closed doors, the wolf behind closed doors, and the bear behind closed doors. I have to stop and say I believe God is going to make your private achievements turn into public triumphs!

Wherever you are at right now may look like waiting time but I believe in the Spirit it is your training time! I know for a fact that I am prophetically uttering a word to someone reading this book even now!

You are reading this book because you have an interest, a pull into the prophetic deep in your spirit, and you may have been in the back, unnoticed, yet humble and serving, and the Lord is looking for you and the anointing will find you.

The anointing is part of the defining of the prophetic, because it is a prophetic anointing that God is placing on many today that will manifest the glories of the Kingdom of God in such a way, that so many will be so astonished at the display of the manifestation of the Kings words!

So the prophetic speaks and causes manifestations by the Spirit of the Lord. The prophetic is not man's ideas, thoughts, assumptions, conjures, familiarities, or anything of the flesh, but it is the divine discourse from the Lord himself through the person by the anointing.

Always remember that the nature of prophecy always exceeds the flesh, and by the flesh I am referring to anything of the natural unrenewed mind and/or of any human origin in this sense. Prophecy may come through the mouth of us, however, it doesn't originate by the mouth of us, prophecy originates from the mouth of God!

Chapter 4

The Importance of the Prophetic

Imagine if there was no voice of God, no Rhema, no prophecy, and no communication from God at all. That would be like going from Malachi all the way to Matthew again, besides the Word of God says to not despise prophecy in 1 Thessalonians 5:20!

The Word of God is clear on the importance of the prophetic, and also as a Prophet myself of the Lord, I can really speak on the importance of the prophetic.

You will learn more about the Prophet himself as we get into Chapter 7 concerning the ministry of the Prophet which ties in with this Chapter you are reading now.

The Prophetic is important for many various reasons but one I would like to point out is that it is important to know the revelation of the truth against darkness.

"The prophetic brings light and revelation to where there was darkness and ignorance of the light of the Kings word."

The prophetic is important because a word is given in a timely matter. There are many times that we are seeking a word from the Lord, or through a Prophet that can come right when the Lord knows it was needed.

However, I would prefer words that I need than words I want to hear. When the Lord speaks, we know that it is always a very timely word. The prophetic brings light and revelation to where there was darkness and ignorance of the light of the Kings word.

Let me just pause and say that this is not just a time for the prophetic, but the Lord is always constantly reassuring it by his Word, and by the proof of the prophetic display that is still happening despite the fight against it.

The prophetic is important because it can bring a word in the midst of another subject that was needed by the hearer at that time. I am sure you have heard preachers while preaching on a subject all of a sudden say the common prophetic phrase "I don't know why I am going this way, or I did not even plan to say this" etc. It is because the Word of the Lord is speaking in a timely way against the path the preacher may have planned.

This is why I have said for over 29 years that I do not preach sermons, I preach the good Kingdom Rhema of the gospel of the Kingdom of God. A sermon again is nothing more than a religious dissertation.

The prophetic helps to show you where you presently are that you may not be willing to see, or even see at all, which is part of what a Prophet will do.

The Bible is the infallible, inspired written Word of God, also called the logos, which means the thoughts of God; however a Rhema spiritually speaking is an inspired utterance from the Lord.

For example, in Article John Section 1 Subsection 1, the word there is logos, an expressed thought, or written word. Now in Article Luke Section 3 Subsection 2, the word that came to John was a Rhema, an uttered word. I believe that there can be a word while a Man or a Woman of God is up ministering and the Spirit of the Lord can just utter something to your spirit or mind where you heard what the minister never said, which came out of the anointing of the Word going forth, or a Word was illuminated to you right on time that stood out to you.

I will let you in on a prophetic knowing and that is the fact the Lord can speak a word through someone without any other single point of reference. This is why that the prophetic is so important as well. The word is inspired by God, so when did God stop inspiring?

This is why we must be careful before saying that was not of God. Jesus told Peter he would deny him. Peter did not have a previous word on this, so there was doubt by Peter when this was spoken to him by Jesus, although it was prophetic by the Lord himself. We believe every prophetic word is necessarily going to be something you knew already, not necessarily.

See this is where a Prophet can see from the other side of the wall and prophesy. A Prophet can get a word in your distance that you have not seen already, or even knew in your present.

Some prophetic warnings you may not have ever known came from prophecy and thank the Lord because the purpose of the warning was to show you what you did not see. A prophetic word can even prepare you for what is to come, and build you for what is your now.

Jesus spoke spirit in John 6:63 (see I gave you a break from the Articles, Section and Subsections), and spirit is not going to always agree with your theology. God is not logical, he is Spirit. We have to stop trying to reduce God to our size to make him like us because if you do that then you do not recognize who he is because you have mentally equalized him as your co-equal, instead of a God we can remain in reverence of.

The prophetic brings glory to God, and his glory alone is important. This is why prophetic people must stay humble and submissive to authority and to the Lord.

This is why Pastors are important and spiritual Fathers are so important because you must not and cannot be a lone ranger because even the lone ranger had a Tonto.

Prophetic people hear the heart of God and the mind of God in such a supernatural way that it exceeds the norm. The prophetic breeds in the glory of the Lord. When the Lord is in the midst, the prophetic can surely flow.

The ability to hear the Lord is so important because you never want to say what the Lord never said. It is important in the prophetic that we totally allow the Lord to flow through us and not us flowing through ourselves.

For example, when prophesying, you may hear someone start off by saying "thus saith the Lord." Now the word thus, is an old English word and that word does not make a prophetic utterance any more divine than just starting off with what the Lord actually has said or is saying. We do not have to use old English terms to convince anyone what the Lord is saying. Sometimes we may hear "and the Lord would say" or "hear the word of the Lord", etc., but the point is to speak what you know he is saying and not add any unnecessary quotes or colloquialisms to it.

We do not have to cook up and add our own seasons and ingredients to what the Lord God is saying; he is the inventor and the creator of all seasonings. This is why reading good books, and getting instructions and training in the prophetic are so important because we must learn the prophetic and the prophetic flow.

We must do all things decently and in order and there is an order to and in the prophetic. For example, if someone is preaching or teaching, you do not just get up while they are delivering and start prophesying, that is out of order.

The reason it is out of order is because God does not interrupt himself!

Prophecy is important because God is our Father and a loving Father loves to speak to his children. You may wonder, well we have the Word of God, the Bible, the Royal Constitution, so why does he still need to speak.

Well the Unites States has a Constitution, so why does the President still need to speak to us? Why do Governors, and Senators, and the people still need to speak?

Our King still speaks today because he still has a Kingdom. Why would a King stop speaking? One way a King rules is by declaring. I wrote this book, but should that stop me from speaking verbally?

This is a time when we need to know what the Lord is saying in this present time. It is great that the Lord can reveal an understanding and an enlightenment of what is happening with the government here presently on earth. It is great that the Lord can still forewarn of things to come and what we should take action in now. It is a great thing that the Lord can speak in our hearts a comforting word, and a word of reassurance to those that need it.

I will never forget the time when my Father told me the Lord showed him a vision of the rapture and the Lord told him you shall go but not now. He told me that he wondered why the Lord showed him this, and the Lord spoke to him and said because you are weak!

This was interesting to me as he was telling me because for the Lord to say you are weak, means you are weak, period. Anything God says is true no matter if you do not see it the way he said it, it is still the truth! So I said wow!

I said wow because my Father prays for hours, fasts for days, stays in the word, shows the demonstration of the Lord in his life, has forgiven everyone who would do something to him futuristically and in the now, he has helped many people, he has encouraged many people, he lives a God-filled life, and the list goes on, and God told him he was weak.

This did not mean that he was weak in the sense of his belief in the Lord or even obeying the Lord, but God knows none of us are as strong as he is and he sees in all of us our strengths and our weaknesses. In other words the Lord was saying no matter what, he sees all, and knows we are still on this earth and have humanistic traits and He is all Spirit and all knowing! Besides in comparison to God, we are all weak!

So my point is that the voice of the Lord is needed in whatever way he chooses to communicate to us. It lets us know he is alive to our situations today, as he was with those of yesterday, and that is a God of love!

My mother is a dreamer, and the Lord has shown her many dreams that have come to pass. Why? It is because the Lord shares information he has to us so we can pray about it. Some dreams are to warn, some dreams are to inform, and some dreams come so we can have an understanding. Some dreams are so we can pray that the Lord will move in a certain direction based on what he shares with us. This is why prayer is so important in the prophetic because prayer does move God.

Isn't it amazing that God had to negotiate with Abraham before destroying Sodom and Gomorrah? It is because he has given us dominion and God is a God of principles. God does not override his own principles!

Since God is a King and has given us dominion on earth to rule, then as we pray we give our King the rights to move on earth on our behalf in agreement and partnership with him. Wow, prayer is so powerful, so we will write a book on prayer as well.

So in what we are talking about here, we should surely see that the prophetic demonstrates the Kings relationship with his royal family, his children.

So as a loving Father, he does not just write letters but calls us every now and then as well. Besides, he lives inside of us, and our bodies are the temple of the Holy Spirit. Can you imagine someone living in the house and not speaking? That would be rude and unbecoming.

It is also rude and unbecoming if we do not speak to him. See prayer is not just you speaking to God. If you are the only one doing the talking then you could be talking to yourself and not really engaging with the Lord.

Prayer is communicating and talking to one another, if it is only one way, then only one is talking and one is listening. I believe the Lord wants to speak to you in prayer, and the problem is that many times we are so quick to end the prayer "in Jesus name amen", that when we get up we are finished and therefore we do not wait to hear his reply.

This is why so many churches have weak prayer meetings because prayer I believe is unfortunately so misunderstood. If we really understood prayer, then how can a meeting where we gather to engage with the Lord in talking, petitioning, etc., be a weak gathering? It has become so religionized that we allowed it to become weak as well. Many of us do not even know that we can even approach the Lord as a Judge in prayer mode and that is another story that we need to understand.

I remember all night shut-ins where we would pray all night and the glory of the Lord would be present and at times a prophetic utterance would come forth, now we have all night sleep-ins instead. Why not give the Lord a call today? It is toll free!

Prophecy is so important because where there is no vision or no prophetic communication then the people perish or have no restraint. Prophecy keeps you aligned. Letting you alone is actually a formula for disaster because there is no relationship of communication.

We then may wonder why is it that all prophetic revelations in communicational displays are not clear to us. This is because the Lord loves fellowship in a relationship. If everything was totally clear you may not seek him or draw near to him. This is why sometimes he may not say something for a while to keep you close to him to get the revelation and/or answer.

Sometimes the Lord will allow us to be in some situations because it will keep you in prayer close to him. Sometimes it is a learning time as well for you.

In Proverbs 25:2, (see I gave you another break) it clearly tells us how the glory of God is to conceal a matter but the glory of Kings is to search it out. God likes when you search him out.

I like how in the book of James it tells us to draw nigh to him and he will draw nigh to us. What a Promise! Then in 1 John 5:14, 15, (ok, now I got to go back to my Article, Sections and Subsections, I am just trying to work with you a little because changing the mindset takes a minute) he tells us if we ask according to his will he hears us and we have the petitions that we ask of him. What a government of Heaven, you can only petition a government, so prayer is proof of the Kings government. Oh I am so excited; ok let me calm down a little.

The prophetic is also important in a way you may not have thought of. It brings the family of God together and closer because it can cause you to share a word with someone else and cause diligence in searching the matter out together in prayer, meditation, discussion and study. See God is so super intelligent, he knows what he is doing.

The prophetic is important also because it can unravel what was not understood by you even in your studying. Have you ever been studying and studying and all of a sudden the revelation of what you been studying suddenly hits you with such understanding? Yes, that's how he does it at times!

Prophecy is also important because it reveals the heart, mind and the purposes that God has concerning a particular thing, person, situation, etc.

Prophecy is important because it positions us. It positions us in our faith to stand on what he says. It is great when the Lord speaks because it gives us the reassurance that no matter what we see, go through, or experience, we have a sure word from the Lord concerning a matter.

I remember a time when I was meditating on the word, and studying to see what the Lord would have me to minister. Then I heard the voice of the Lord clearly say to me to tell the people to say "Holy Ghost let your fire fall." So, when I was introduced and presented, I told the people I have no message to preach but the Lord told me to have everyone say Holy Ghost let your fire fall. Believe me, it fell, was seen, was felt, and the manifestations of healings were happening on so many levels. The Pastors wife had some sort of growth coming up on her back and the Fire of the Lord healed it right in the service.

I had a dream once at the age of about 14 that there was a lady in a wheel chair and I looked and said "fire" and she got up out of the wheel chair. Now this dream was years before the Holy Spirit told me to say let his fire fall in that service.

This prophetic dream that I did not understand then was revealed that night in the service and ever since then I realized that the Lord has given me a ministry of fire. Now I say fire all the time and the fire of the Spirit of God always comes and manifests whenever I say it one way or the other.

What amazed me was I had never heard or saw anyone say fire. I would say fire, and this still happens to this day, people would hit the floor because of the power individually or if I say it to a group of people standing and the wave of His Majesty, the Kings glory, would hit so hard none of them can or could stand. I have seen so many miraculous happenings when I say fire!

Then one day after ministering, I turned on the TV which I rarely watch to this day and Pastor Benny Hinn was saying fire and people were falling out as well. I said wow, another one saying fire. It is a powerful manifestation I must admit.

The prophetic positions us in patience because the word can cause us to wait until it happens in the midst of what we are facing.

I remember times as I am sure which many of us can relate to, that I wanted to just give up on everything but the Lord would keep reminding me of a sure word, or words he had spoken to me, through me, and even from others, and it confirmed my purpose which is another thing that the prophetic does, it confirms your purpose.

It is also amazing when several prophecies tell you all similar things especially when not one of them knows you and all these prophetic utterances are coming from people that do not even know each other as well. That is just amazing to me.

The prophetic builds your faith in a big way because there are some prophetic utterances that come through where there is no way no one could of known the information but the Lord and therefore your faith builds as well as the recognition of how much the Lord loves you to reveal such a thing to you.

Chapter 5

The Different Realms of the Prophetic

This brings us to the so many different realms of the prophetic which can be pretty exhaustive but the purpose of this book is to just give you a good prophetic edge and jump into more of understanding the prophetic from a Kingdom point of view.

The prophetic is indeed extensive and can prove complicated, but we want to bring you into the understanding of it enough where there is a deeper enrichment in your prophetic life.

A realm then is a kingdom and it is also a sphere of activity in which something occurs, so I believe that this is a good word choice for understanding this next phase of the prophetic.

There are several realms or expressions of the prophetic that I want to discuss. The first realm of the prophetic that I want to discuss is very important and that is the scriptures.

The Scriptures

In Article 2 Peter Section 1 Subsection 20, it says that no prophecy of the scripture is of any private interpretation. The context this scripture is surrounded by makes it clear to us that the scriptures or even the different prophetic words of the scriptures, or their words are not by what they heard of as fables, these men were eye witnesses, and heard and seen by themselves personally.

These words are not made up, and scripture in itself is totally prophetic and has its origin by God himself. What a blessing to know it is of and from the Lord! Oh the power of the Word of the Lord! Ok, let's move on.

Prophecy is as a bright light shining in a dark place. Scriptures say thy Word is a lamp unto my feet, and also the bible clearly states how scriptures are God breathed. Another word for this is theopneustos in the Greek, which means inspired by God or breathed on by God.

We see this same word used in scripture, in the Constitution of Heaven in 2 Timothy 3:16 as the word inspired. So therefore scriptures itself is prophetic, for the Word declares that holy men spoke as they were moved by God, not themselves.

The written Word of God is surely prophetic because it is God breathed and communicated by God through men, for men.

So the Lord wanted us to know his plan, purpose, will, desire, design, and about the fact that he is King, he has a Kingdom and we are his Royal family all in the prophetic Word of God.

The scriptures are so amazing because you can get so many Rhemas from the Logos. We must learn that when there is a scripture that we see in the Word, we must believe and understand the power of the Word of God.

In Article Luke Section 1 Subsection 37, it says *"For with God nothing shall be impossible"*. The angel is expressing that whatever God says, it is possible even when it does not seem possible to man, but there is more to stretch here concerning the Word of the Lord.

Now the word "nothing" in this verse is the word Rhema! In other words, God's word is so powerful that no word of God will come to you that does not have the capability in and of itself to bring to pass what it came to say!

This is now further explained in another section of his word in Article Isaiah Section 55 Subsection 11, let's read it.

It says *"So shall my word be that goeth forth out of my mouth: it shall not return unto me void, but it shall accomplish that which I please, and it shall prosper in the thing whereto I sent it."*

In this verse, "word" in the Hebrew here is the word "dabar", which means utterance (now keep in mind this is referring to the utterance of the Lord, or his word). The word for "void" is the Greek word "reyqam", and it means in empty condition without effect. So his Word will not return in empty condition without effect! It will accomplish and prosper into the thing where he sent it. It never mentioned faith here!

Faith or the currency of Heaven comes by hearing, so hearing invites and receives faith, and hearing by the Word of God. So the word has a faith of its own to work, but do you have the faith to work the word for you?

See faith is so powerful with the Word, but the Word already has a faith with it, so we must mix our measure of faith that he has already given us, to the faith that the Word already has, and the faith along with your hearing to make it work for you.

When I mention the term currency of Heaven we understand that governments here use currency, on earth it is money in Heaven it is faith.

So the Word of God is the thoughts of God written and many may wonder why it is in different styles of writing if it is all from God. This is when we must understand that whatever style the Lord wanted to express himself in, he would choose who wrote according to that flow of expression. Like David was poetic and flowed in musical lyrics, and so forth.

So, the Word of God according to Hebrews 4:12 tell us that it is alive! The scriptures are his written living words!

Another realm of the prophetic that I want to discuss is the Spirit of prophecy.

The Spirit of Prophecy

The Spirit of prophecy is mentioned several times in the book of Revelation. If we look at Article Revelation Section 19 Subsection 10, the later part says "......*for the testimony of Jesus is the spirit of prophecy.*"

The word testimony here is the Greek word *marturia* which simply means a testimony or what one testifies. So the Spirit of Prophecy is what Jesus testifies. Now Spirit here is the Greek word *pneuma* which refers to the Holy Spirit.

So, the Spirit of prophecy is the testimony of Christ through the Holy Spirit. So that which is prophetic in nature will always bring glory to the Lord, and this is pretty evident in Article 1 Corinthians Section 12 Subsection 3 where it says *"Wherefore I give you to understand, that no man speaking by the Spirit of God calleth Jesus accursed: and that no man can say that Jesus is the Lord, but by the Holy Ghost."*

In other words, when we are speaking under the supernatural divine utterance, direction and inspiration of the Spirit of the Lord, the Holy Spirit can't say anything bad concerning Jesus.

So let's summarize all of this a little more to bring good clarity to this prophetic realm. The Spirit of prophecy represents the Holy Spirit speaking and always exalting Jesus in nature. The Spirit of prophecy here is referring to the Holy Spirit being prophetic in nature exalting Christ.

True prophetic anointings will never degrade the Lord. Keep in mind that the Holy Spirit brings forth the prophetic voice of God.

In Article Psalm Section 110 Subsection 1 it says *"The LORD said unto my Lord, Sit thou at my right hand, until I make thine enemies thy footstool."* The interesting thing is how Jesus referred to this scripture in Article Matthew Section 22 Subsection 43 ...he asks *how then doth David in spirit call him Lord.* The word *in*, actually means by. So Jesus is referring to this testimony of Jesus, the Spirit of prophecy, was by the Spirit of the Lord.

The Spirit of God brings a realm of anointing that is prophetic in essence as well as in nature, and when in that environment or around anointed Prophets of God, I believe at that time that almost anyone can prophesy depending on the weight of that specific glory that is present.

The Spirit of prophecy will use anyone he wants to administer his word.

So a spoken or written testimony here represents the Spirit of prophecy and it will always bring change. The testimony of Jesus has the ability to bring and cause about change.

In 1 Samuel 10 we see how the Prophet prophesied to Saul and told him the Spirit of the Lord will come upon him to prophesy, and it tells us how he came into the company of Prophets and we read that his heart was changed as a result of prophesying.

The next realm I want to discuss is the gift of prophecy.

The Gift of Prophecy

The gift of prophecy is given by the Holy Spirit and we know this from the supernatural 9 gifts of the Spirit mentioned in 1 Corinthians 12. The gift of prophecy is the ability and anointing to prophecy.

Now we must understand that the gift of prophecy is not the office of a Prophet. The gift of prophecy and the Prophet are two different manifestations of gifts. In Ephesians 4: 8-13, it discusses the ministry gifts. These ministry gifts Jesus gave to the Church are not the same as the gift of the Spirit here in 1 Corinthians 12.

In 1 Corinthians 12, these are the gifts of the Holy Spirit, but in Ephesians, these are the ministry gifts from Jesus. A Prophet would have the gift of prophecy but just because you prophesy, it does not mean or make you a Prophet.

We will get into the office and ministry of the Prophet in detail in Chapter 7.

So the gift of prophecy enables a person to speak words of edification, exhortation and comfort according to Article 1 Corinthians Section 14 Subsection 3 where it says "*But he that prophesieth speaketh unto men to edification, and exhortation, and comfort.*"

So as you can see here that the gift of prophecy does not fore-tell the future, it forth-tells. It's a supernatural utterance in a tongue that is understood by the hearers to edify, exhort and comfort, not predict the future. Now it is very important to understand that futuristic events can come forward through the verbal utterance but that is when another gift is used in conjunction with the vehicle of prophecy.

For example, the gift of the word of knowledge reveals a portion of things of the past, and present of a person, place, or thing. It is a word from the Lord, which only denotes a partial knowledge of something.

So if I was to go forth prophetically and say to you, yesterday you were praying at 3:00 pm and the Lord heard your prayers, then that is a prophetic utterance relating to the past through the gift of prophecy verbally since the gift of prophecy would be a supernatural utterance given verbally.

So as we can see here clearly that two gifts of the Spirit would be working in operation together, the gift of prophecy as the utterance vehicle and the word of knowledge as the facts are stated concerning the past or present.

Now please note that the gift of the word of wisdom is not the gift of wise sayings because Solomon was wise and you can get wisdom by getting on your knees and asking for it, so it is the gift of the word of wisdom.

It's also not natural wisdom because all of these nine gifts are supernatural. Now, the revelatory gift of the word of wisdom will always point and reveal a portion of the purpose and will of God which is usually futuristic in essence.

In Acts 9:10-16, we see the gift of the word of knowledge and the word of wisdom both in operation. In Article Luke Section 2 Subsections 25-35, we see here that Simeon prophesied to Mary concerning Jesus because he spoke prophetically.

With the woman at the well, Jesus was used in the gift of the word of knowledge because he stated things concerning her past and present. He was used in the word of knowledge because she testified and said come see a man who told me everything I did which was past and he explained about the time is coming concerning where they would worship, which details the mind and plan of God, the word of wisdom, futuristically speaking!

She also perceived he was a Prophet and he never corrected that statement because he was a Prophet!

Now please take note that edification always builds up and it also always promotes growth. Now exhortation encourages, comforts, consoles or alleviates grief but this is supernaturally.

So therefore a word spoken under the inspiration of the Holy Spirit that edifies, encourages and also comforts, is the simple expression of the gift of prophecy.

In Luke 1, we see that Zacharias prophesied and it was indeed very edifying, comforting and exhorting.

Paul encourages us to prophesy and to covet this gift because it is so valuable to the church in building the church.

I will add that even when someone is speaking in tongues as a message where the gift of interpretation of tongues is administered afterwards, that also equals prophecy. The reason it is also considered prophecy is because the tongues was a message if it was interpreted to edify those that are hearers which would obviously equal to a prophetic word!

This is why it is important that we be so sensitive to the Holy Spirit of prophecy so we can know when someone is speaking in tongues is praying or if there is a prophetic message coming forth. The anointing to know this answer is not based on the high volume of the person that is speaking in tongues because volume is not anointing, volume is loudness of sound. So do not let volume make you feel or believe it is a message or someone shaking, etc. It is important to distinguish what is what because if not, we will bring confusion, or even possibly a halt to the continuation and full counsel of what the Lord is doing and or even saying.

One way that you can know if the person speaking in tongues is giving a message or if it is a prayer is by just being quiet and being very sensitive by allowing the Holy Spirit to inform you by illuminating your heart to know if there is something more than just this person speaking in tongues and often times the Holy Spirit will bring a move or a blanket of quietness over everyone so that we can hear the interpretation of the tongues spoken, not translation, but the meaning of what was spoken in tongues.

Another thing that is important to remember is that we all prophesy according to the portion of our faith, in other words as you release a prophetic word into the atmosphere, it can keep going according to your faiths release, but please do not go past faith or you will enter into flesh.

Another realm of the prophetic is the ministry gift of the Prophet.

The Prophet

I will not dive too much into the ministry gift of the Prophet because that is for a later chapter in this book but the office of the Prophet is one of the realms of the prophetic because the Prophet does indeed prophesy, but the revelations given to the Prophet is way more extensive than just having the gift of prophecy.

The Prophet is a minister of the gospel, and they do preach the Word of God. The Prophet is one who God uses in so many various ways to administer the prophetic and they are chosen by God.

They have a special grace, or anointing to prophetically utter the deep things of God because of the way the revelation is given to them.

In Ephesians 4:11, as well as 1 Corinthians 12:38, (going back and forth from Articles to what many are used to, trying to break you in little by little still) we see the mention of the Prophet the Lord has placed in the Church.

So the Prophet is a very important part of the prophetic for obvious reasons and many unfortunately in the church do not believe that Prophets exist.

It is dangerous to not believe that Prophets are still here today because Jesus clearly gave them as gifts to his church, and if you reject a gift, then you have not received the gift and what makes a gift complete is receiving it. If there are no Prophets today, then there are no Apostles, Pastors, Evangelists or Teachers either.

As a matter of fact, you do not even hear people say Teacher Reed, or Teacher Cantaloupe, but you hear Pastor so and so, etc. It is because the Teacher is marked by revelation and gives illumination to you as another ministry gift, and the enemy really hates the Teacher ministry because they bring you into understandings and revelations to such degrees that makes you want to operate in that teaching to apply it right away.

There are definitely Prophets today just like there are Pastors today. We need to embrace the office ministry of the Prophet and the ministry of the Apostle as well because they are ministry gifts given by the Lord, and if we reject the gift, we reject the giver of the gifts.

Many times the church does not value the Apostle or Prophet because they do not understand those ministry office gifts due to them not being taught about it unfortunately. This is why teaching the true Word of God is so imperative without the religious additives that taint the truth of the Word.

The Prophet also carries a great responsibility that many may think is so glorious from their viewpoint but please trust me, it comes with a whole lot of time, devotion, studying, praying, meditation of his word, fasting, learning, rebuke, hurts, being forsaken, and the list goes on.

I have heard many people come to me and repeatedly say I want the anointing that you have, and I always think or and sometimes I would say, no you do not. The anointing costs! We want the anointing of the Prophet and do not even want to carry the bag of and for the Prophet!

Simon wanted the gift so bad that he wanted to buy it, but the gift is not bought, it is given. The Prophet again operates in a higher realm than one who just has the gift of prophecy.

The Prophets ministry is not a spooky ministry, but a ministry that should walk in humility, and submission. Prophets are viewed all kinds of ways because people do not understand the ministry of the Prophet.

Other realms of the prophetic are more dealt with on how the prophetic is displayed and we will get into that in the next chapter, so let's go there.

Chapter 6

The Different Displays of the Prophetic

In discussing the different displays of the prophetic, we will see different ways the prophetic is manifested to give us a better understanding on how the King of Kings in his divine intelligence manifests the prophetic. I want to emphasize that prophecy is also based on the need for God to say something. When God wants to speak or communicate, trust me, he knows how to do so and when.

Timing is so very important in the prophetic because a word spoken in due season is good. The prophetic timing has to be known even in a Prophets life, but we will get into that soon, I am going ahead of myself here.

We must learn to not take it upon ourselves to adamantly say he only moves this way or that way because he moves any way he wants but there are manifestations in the Word that we can see that are all different.

For instance, the ways that the gifts of the Spirit are displayed and manifested, the way healing is manifested, the way teaching is manifested, the way preaching is manifested, and this is why I love how the Word declares in Article 1 Corinthians Section 12 Subsections 4-7 explains it.

It says "*Now there are diversities of gifts, but the same Spirit* (all by the same Holy Spirit). *And there are differences of administrations,* (there are different ways it is administered or dispensed) *but the same Lord. And there are diversities of operations,* (different ways it is operated or activated) *but it is the same God which worketh all in all But the manifestation of the Spirit is given to every man to profit withal.*"

So there are so many different displays of the prophetic that it would be impossible to list all of them, but again we are not trying to be very exhaustive in this book, we are just trying to give you a good portion of a Kingdom understanding of the prophetic.

Preaching under Divine Inspiration

One way the prophetic is displayed is through preaching the Word. Preaching is proclaiming, and if you are a minister of the gospel proclaiming, or ministering the Word of God under divine inspiration, then that alone is a form of the prophetic because it is prophesying the Word under the inspiration of the Word, Jesus! It is amazing that you can be ministering the Word and go to a whole completely different word within the word. This happens often under the divine unction of the Holy Spirit prophetically.

There are many times while I am ministering that the Lord would give me a prophetic word for someone, and then I would go right back to ministering.

The Multitude of Counsellors

The prophetic is also given through the multitude of counsel, where there is safety. People unfortunately miss this. I have heard people say I need confirmation, and so the Lord allows several people to tell you similar things.

I remember when a time when I was constantly before the Lord asking for instructions and directions, etc., that all of a sudden in a matter of a few days, several people came with instructions and counsel who were all saying pretty much the same thing, and from that way the Lord was speaking. I was honestly expecting him to just tell me in an audible voice, or through a certain scripture, or maybe through a dream, etc., but he spoke to me in counsel through other people.

In Article Acts Section 15, there was a dispute over if they should they circumcise or not circumcise. They determined that they should go to Jerusalem to the Apostles and Elders about this question. After they discussed it, counsel was given and reached, AND IT SEEMED GOOD TO THE HOLY GHOST AND THEM and then they wrote letters addressing this issue. The Holy Spirit is involved in godly counsel, and that is another way the prophetic is displayed.

"The Word of Counsel is always better than the World of Counsel because the World of Counsel will never be prophetic like the Word of Counsel!"

Counsel or advice from a multitude of godly people is great because the multitude will confirm the counsel by repeat. The Word of God is the best counsel, or counsel, of the Word. As a matter of fact, we should be careful going to the ungodly for counsel on matters of destiny, purpose, and the things of God in your life for obvious reasons. You see the Word of counsel is always better than the world of counsel because the world of counsel will never be prophetic like the Word of counsel!

The devil is the god of this world, or world systems, so his children cannot give you Word advice, only world advice when it comes to the prophetic.

I like in Article Proverbs Section 24 Subsection 6 where it basically explains before you engage in war, or decisions, get wise counselling on it by multitudes.

Let's move into another way the prophetic is displayed.

Dreams

Another way that the prophetic is displayed is through dreams. Pilate's wife had a dream for Pilate, the governor, not to have anything to do with Jesus. After all a lamb is sacrificed by a priest, so God had it where the Priest Caiaphas was involved, but that is another message.

The Magi had a dream not to return to king Herod, Joseph in the New Testament had a dream to not divorce Mary, and yet he had another dream to flee to Egypt, and Joseph in the Old Testament had a dream revealing the future, Daniel had dreams about the Kingdom of God in Daniel 7.

We see more prophetic dreams when Abraham in Genesis 15 dreamed of Israel's bondage, and concerning their deliverance with wealth, and his own death. In Numbers 12, God admits that he deals with Prophets also in dreams.

Please note that every dream that a person dreams is not always necessarily from the Lord our God. In Ecclesiastes 5, it mentions that dreams come from the multitude of business in a day. Dreams can come from situations that stayed on your mind before going to sleep.

However, dreams are just another vehicle that the prophetic comes through. Prophetic dreams can come to relay a truth, a warning of the future, instructions, they can show you yourself, they can encourage, they can show you Gods plan; and they can even confirm a promise to you from a prophecy.

However, remember even with certain dreams, the multitude of counsellors. Everyone is not anointed to interpret dreams so you must be careful who you take a dream to if you do not understand the dream.

In Article Genesis Section 41, we see how Joseph interpreted pharaoh's dream, and thank God that he was remembered. You would be surprised how God can use you, and someone remembers and that remembrance saves you, and others. God is going to cause you to be remembered!

So here it is, Joseph interprets pharaohs dream and was then favoured. It is also of note to notice and understand that the fact that he dreamed the same thing twice meant it was established by God and should shortly come to pass.

When you keep on having the same dream, usually there is a reason and a meaning, and it could be that the Lord is trying to communicate something to you. Pay attention to that.

We know that dreams are from God as well because God is giving Joseph the interpretation of the dream. As a result, look at all of the favour that was bestowed and given to Joseph all because of a dream and the interpretation.

I really like how it reads in Article Daniel Section 2 when King Nebuchadnezzar had a dream and forgot what the dream was about and therefore he was troubled. So he calls his astrologer, astronomers, magicians, and sorcerers who thought they were cool because they figured they could interpret the dream.

However, the king got deep on them and said it left me, so you have to tell me what I dreamed and the interpretation thereof and if not, you shall be cut in pieces and your houses shall be made a dunghill or in other words, reduced to rubble as a garbage dump! Can you imagine that? What a threat and punishment if you do not tell the dream that left, and to add insult to injury, interpret it as well!

They replied that no one on earth can show the kings matter. So the king decreed to slay all the wise men of Babylon!

Daniel desired of the king that he would be given time to tell him the dream and the interpretation of it. So he goes to his three companions so they can pray with him so that the King of Kings can tell him the dream in a night vision, or possibly dream the king's dream that was revealed which was a secret. See the secret things belong to the Lord but he does nothing unless he reveals it to his Prophets (Amos 3:7). Look at God!

Daniel was brought to the king by the captain and when the king asked Daniel can he tell him, I love Daniels response. Daniel said, none of those you asked could tell you, but the God in heaven revealeth secrets, and he boldly proclaimed to the king his dream and the interpretation of the dream!

Notice the king wondered in his mind what shall come to pass, and Daniel confirmed that the Lord gave the king the answers in his dreams. You see, the Lord does communicate prophetically through dreams.

I love how the Lord was letting a king know that the King's Kingdom shall come and be the everlasting Kingdom! Glory to the King!

As a result, the king admitted that Daniels God is the Lord of all Kings, and favour was bestowed on Daniel, and his friends were hooked up too. Our King is a mighty King and he speaks to us in dreams as well.

This is why your Pastor is so very important so you can tell the Pastor your dream and see what the counsel or possibly the word of the Lord is concerning that particular dream.

God has graced some of his saints to interpret dreams because he gives dreams! Why would he grace with an interpretation for dreams, if there is no giver of dreams?

Visions

Another way the prophetic is displayed is through visions.

Let me emphasize that dreams and visions are not the same. A dream is when you are asleep and whether it is pictures, or motions, or conversations, etc., you are not physically aware because you are asleep. You are not consciously awake. A vision is when you are seeing what the Lord is showing you while you are awake, and not sleep.

There is a gift of the Spirit mentioned in 1 Corinthians 12 that mentions the gift of the discerning of spirits. Not the gift of discernment as I have heard many say down through the years, I am referring to the biblical mentioning of the gift of the discerning of spirits.

This gift is part of the revelatory gifts because there is something God is revealing and showing you.

The gift of discerning of spirits is when there is revelation to you by the Holy Spirit on the kind of spirit that is in operation in the manifestation of anything that is supernatural in nature. It is a supernatural gift that distinguishes spirits. This gift reveals if it is the influence of God, the devil, or the flesh.

Many times when hearing about certain dreams, this gift can be active to tell you if this dream was of the Lord or not.

There are different types of visions. Prophets have visions, but so do people that are prophetic as God chooses. Prophetic people are people who God uses prophetically in the manner he chooses, which again does not make you a Prophet.

One type of vision is a supernatural insight in the Spirit by your spirit. You remember when Paul fell off his horse on the road to Damascus? No you do not remember that because the bible never said that. See how the church has done an excellent job in teaching errors?

Usually at about noon, devout Jewish men prayed standing up and they got that from King David when he mentions how he prayed in the morning, noon, and evening in Psalm 55:16-17. So it is at midday, light outside, but the Light of Christ the King shines upon him and communicates with him in Acts 9. This was a supernatural insight by his spirit because he was physically blinded for three days.

Another type of vision is called an open vision. That is where you can hear and see in the spirit realm with your physical eyes still open and your senses are fully in tack unsuspended.

In Article Amos Section 8 Subsection 1, we see that the King showed Prophet Amos a basket of fruit, and then went on to explain the meaning of what was shown and seen.

In the book of Revelation, we see John had many open visions, and then in Acts 10 Peter had an open vision because the Lord told him to kill and eat. The interesting thing about this open vision is that he could have participated in it since he was told to kill and eat. In the book of Revelation, John ate a book and described how it even tasted, so in open visions, nothing is suspended.

Another type of vision is when you are in a trance. In a trance, all of your physical senses are suspended and you are more conscious of the things God is showing you, whether they're images or pictures.

In Acts 22:17, Paul said he was in a trance and saw the Lord talking to him, and he responded to the Lord, but he was still in a trance, so it is in the Spirit, and not in flesh.

Keep in mind that visions are still divine revelations. There is something the King is showing you, and wants you to know and see. It is important that we do not portray an image in our minds on our own and proclaim that it is the Lord.

Sometimes we may want something so very bad and have an image in our minds and claim it is the Lord. The Lord allows you to have an imagination, and that is why you can imagine whatever you want to imagine.

You can have a free vacation by just imagining you are where you want to be, but that is an image you have placed there. Whatever you place in your mind on your own is not a vision from the Lord. When he communicates, he is communicating to you, not you communicating to you.

Mini – Revelational Visions & Thoughts

Let me say that a lot of times we can have a mini revelational vision or thought where God splashes a quick image in our spirit, or perhaps to our mind, and all of a sudden there is a great understanding on something you did not understand before.

This also can be a message where you are about to prophesy and something appears to you, and it is real quick, maybe even a millisecond, and it is gone. I know by experience and even talking to others that this happens.

God can bring a sudden inner thought without any outside contribution, self-meditation or stimulus to you that you did not bring to you. It just comes to you as the Holy Spirit brings it to you.

I like how Peter answered Jesus and Jesus replied, flesh and blood has not revealed this to you, but my Father which is in

Heaven according to Article Matthew Section 16. This was an interruptive suddenly that came to Peter.

You may have heard the Hebrew word naba which means to bubble up in reference to the prophetic flowing, well this was a naba. It flowed out of Peter.

I like Article Proverbs Section 20 Subsection 27 where it says *"The spirit of man is the candle of the LORD, searching all the inward parts of the belly."* Then John 7:38 tells us that out of our bellies shall flow rivers of living waters. See, he speaks from within us!

Out of your belly shall flow rivers of living waters! Jesus did what he saw his Father do. How did he see his Father? He ministered from a heavenly position on earth.

Let's look at Article John Section 3 Subsection 13. It says *"And no man hath ascended up to heaven, but he that came down from heaven, even the Son of man which is in heaven."* He is saying that he was ministering from a heavenly position because he was on earth speaking to John, yet indicating he was in heaven. Well, did not Paul say that we are seated in heavenly places?

We must minister from where we sit, not where we stand. In other words, minister from your heavenly seat, not from your earthly circumstances. Of course we can minister out of our circumstances from an experiential point of view, but not from a defeated point of view.

So he is ministering from Heaven by his Spirit to us. A Lot of times when I am ministering it is from a heavenly position because it is like I am not on earth while receiving from heaven. My wife can always tell when this is happening to me, somehow she just knows.

There are times when I am prophesying to people that an image would come to my mind and I will express that image and the person is shocked because there was no way I could have known that, but I do not ignore these images that quickly come to my mind because I know where I draw from.

I will throw this in, the more a Prophet looks, the more a Prophet sees!

So we know that every thought is not from God because he tells us to cast down every thought that is against the knowledge of God in 2 Corinthians 10:4-5. So every thought is not of God, so I repent for the thoughts I own, not the ones I do not! However, this is yet another prophetic communication that God does bring to us.

Keep in mind also that God can speak to you to chastise you, speak to you for others, speak to you to confirm your relationship with him, to edify you, or for any reason in any way he wants. Never hinder how he speaks by forming how you will choose to accept how he will speak.

Knowing the voice of God in the prophetic is so important because you cannot release his word to someone else if you do not know his voice your own self.

The Holy Spirit resides in your spirit so it is important to know where his flow comes from, so you can be aware of your spirit. This is another reason why speaking in tongues is so important because it edifies you, and flows from within you.

The Holy Spirit will unction you to function you to speak in tongues as he gives the ability for you to do so, but it comes from the flow within.

We must not think that the Lord is speaking to us all day long, and every single minute of the day in a conversation. I have heard people say the Lord speaks to them all day. If that was the case, how did we all make bad decisions if he is speaking all day long to us? We must be careful that we are not speaking and thinking it is him all the time.

"If you talk a little lower we might hear God Speak, because if you are talking all the time, when and how can we hear him?"

Then there are times that we talk so much we never know what God is saying, so if you talk a little lower we might here God speak, because if you are talking all the time, when and how can we hear him?

Even when we pray we always want to hear from him, but we are doing all the talking, so how could we know when he is speaking?

Impressions & Perceptions

Another way the prophetic is revealed is through impressions and perceptions. Keep in mind that impressions, thoughts, imaginations, perceptions, and the like, must be agreeable to the Word of God, the Constitution of Heaven. At the same time as mentioned in Chapter 4, there are some prophetic words that have no point of reference.

Bananas are not mentioned in the Constitution of Heaven, but we do know for a fact that bananas exist. We cannot say that bananas are not real because the Bible does not mention it.

Just like we mentioned about Peter not knowing that he would deny Christ in Chapter 4, we must understand that if the Bible does not mention every way the prophetic is revealed, it does not mean that the ways that God chooses to reveal himself is not of God. If we were to know of everything Jesus did, the world could not contain the books and that is in the Bible!

We must understand that any prophetic way the Lord reveals himself will not necessarily agree to your norm. This is why I say we cannot assume how God will speak because you do not know all the ways God can speak.

His thoughts are not our thoughts, after all he is King, Creator, and you know that I can go on, and on. Here God promises Abraham a son, and then waits all those years until he has one, and then after all of that God tells him to sacrifice him!

There are things the Lord does that we are not always going to understand, and that is where and when, we have to be like Abraham who never staggered at the promises of God, so God increased his faith.

A lot of times with our tiny little minds, what God says can seem senseless and even contradictory, but he knows all things, and we do not. So we accept whatever he says and does.

I have heard people use the term hunch. They would say I cannot explain it, but I got a hunch, and a lot of times those hunches are correct. No proven evidence, just a hunch, or a feeling, or an impression. God speaks in many ways.

A prophetic impression is a knowing or even a feeling in your spirit formed without evidence, or a knowing without proof that just hits you. It is an intuitive knowing. God can give you a feeling that is through our emotions. You could be praying for someone and feel a feeling of weight for example and the Lord is letting you know this person is burdened.

You could be looking for a particular job and you are wondering if this is the correct choice and there is just a feeling of a no, verses a yes, or just an uncomfortable feeling that this is not the right choice. It is an inward witness in and to your spirit. We say impressions and perceptions because they are so closely related.

A prophetic perception is knowing, seeing and recognizing according to the Hebrew word "nakar", and this word is used concerning Nehemiah.

Nehemiah perceived in Nehemiah 6 that those that were sent to him to persuade him to go into the house of the Lord (going into the house of the Lord seemed right) were not sent by God, for he would not have finished the wall had he followed and listened to their letters.

Another Hebrew word used in 2 Kings 4:9 is the word "yada", where the woman perceived in her heart and then told her husband that this man is a Prophet of God. This word yada has the same meaning which is to know. She just simply knew by this man passing by.

The word perceive in the Greek with the woman at the well is interesting because she told Jesus that she perceived he was a Prophet. The word here is theoreo, which means to look, behold and discern. This is recorded in Article John Section 4 Subsection 19.

There is another Greek word used for when Jesus perceived what people were thinking in Mark Chapter 2. It is the Greek word Epiginosko, which carries even a stronger meaning. This word means to know thoroughly and accurately.

In Article Mark Section 2 Subsections 3-8 it says *"And they come unto him, bringing one sick of the palsy, which was borne of four. And when they could not come nigh unto him for the press, they uncovered the roof where he was: and when they had broken it up, they let down the bed wherein the sick of the palsy lay. When Jesus saw their faith, he said unto the sick of the palsy, Son, thy sins be forgiven thee. But there was certain of the scribes sitting there, and reasoning in their hearts, Why doth this man thus speak blasphemies? Who can forgive sins but God only? And immediately when Jesus perceived in his spirit that they so reasoned within themselves, he said unto them, why reason these things in your heart?"*

Here we see that Jesus perceived in his spirit what they were even thinking! This perception was in his spirit, where the rivers flow!

In Acts 27, Paul perceived their lives would be in danger and the ship would be in danger as well, but they did not listen. Then all of a sudden Euroclydon, which was a strong cyclone, then came, and the ship was in trouble, and Paul told them that they should have listened to him. The centurion wanting to keep them from killing the prisoners which would have included Paul, was not willing for this to happen to Paul, and therefore came against their purpose, for Paul's purpose!

Thank God that Paul had a purpose because purpose will stop death once you lock onto it and hold onto it!

Keep in mind that although feelings are used by God in some of these instances, feelings and emotions are not the primary indicators of facts either. As we grow we know!

So we could sum up by saying impressions are laid upon your spirit, and your feelings can be involved and perceptions are knowing's in your heart. Knowing this is so very important to understanding the moves of the prophetic flow. By knowing this, we can understand some details of the prophetic.

When the Lord gives you an impression, it may not even last long, but you must go with it when you know it is the Lord because some impressions are life savers. Have you ever been driving and you get an impression not to go down a certain street, or do not go this way or that way? It could have been that there would be an accident, or something dangerous was about to happen.

I remember a time I was on my way to school and I saw the weather report on television indicating a sunny day, no rain, but I had an impression to bring my umbrella despite the report. I got to school and everyone there thought I was crazy to bring my umbrella. Like Noah, I told them it was going to rain and sure enough right before class dismissed at the end of the day....well let's just say, I did not get wet.

In Romans 8, it tells us that his Spirit bears witness with our spirits that we are the children of God, and God does speak to his children.

God can speak to you in an audible voice, of which I have heard a few times. He can speak to you through certain signs.

Isaiah 7:14 clearly tells us that the virgin birth of Jesus was a sign! The King did not let the resurrection be a sign because many would have said he was not really dead, but a virgin having a child, now that is a sign! It is amazing that the Lord spoke to Azar and told him to ask for a sign.

Another sign that he used was about the swaddling clothes that baby Jesus at that time was wrapped in because he is not a baby anymore, Praise the Lord!

The swaddling clothes as a sign was told in Luke 2 by the angel to the shepherds. They were told they would find a babe wrapped in swaddling clothes lying in a manger. In verses 15 and 16 they said let us go now, and they came with haste to where he was because swaddling clothes did not stay on a baby for long.

I will never forget when the Lord was sending me to preach the gospel of the Kingdom of God five years later after he called me to preach, I asked for a sign.

I looked up into the heavens and with my left hand I pointed to a star. Then I changed and pointed to another, with my left hand, and then to another and finally stopped at one. Then with my right hand, I pointed to one, and then another, and finally settled upon one location where I was pointing.

I then said "Lord if you are really sending me to preach, then let the star I am pointing to with my left hand land exactly where I am pointing with my right hand. Then lo, and behold, it shot across the sky and stopped right where my right hand was pointing!

Then I went upstairs to my room, still living with my parents at the time, and after praying in tongues for an hour, the Lord Jesus himself appeared to me in an open vision and spoke with me concerning ministry and my life. I was and am still amazed from that experience with the Lord.

I do not encourage that you ask the Lord for signs but he has and can use them. You do not want to say things like, Lord if this is your will let the clock on the wall fall. Not a good sign because then you are relying on happenings and possible chances that may not even be God. God has many ways of getting our attention, and he is not a God of failure.

He can speak to you through a still small voice which almost resembles the voice of your conscious. Of course he speaks to you through the Word of God itself. He can speak to you through a conversation with others. He can speak to you through an angelic visitation.

He can speak through music playing by anointed musicians. I have heard music and words just came to me exalting the Lord, or even ministering to myself.

He can speak to you through a song interpreted through your own self as you sing in tongues.

Job 33:14 says something that is so true, it says, *"For God speaketh once, yea twice, yet man perceiveth it not."* In other words God speaks often but man does not regard it, or misses it.

Even the heavens declare his glory, so we cannot put how he speaks in a box according to how we will accept it and if it does not fit our ways, then we think it cannot be God. Be open to the voice and ways of God.

As I am writing this book, the Lord just brought something to my mind and memory. As I was wondering other ways he does speak without being to exhaustive because no one can cover every single way he speaks. I thought of when I was a young child. My sister and I would act like we were having service. I was the preacher and she and her dolls would be in the congregation as I would put a blanket over me to represent the preachers robe and I would preach.

I recalled how I would act like I was on radio as a gospel DJ, and record announcements from one cassette to another, and record songs, and the weather and compile it together and listen to my radio broadcast. As a matter of fact I remember what I called it. WBGS and for me it stood for Worlds Best Gospel Sounds! I used to have a lot of fun on that station and acted as though it was real.

I recalled how I would write out many pages as though I was writing a book, about different subjects from the Bible at age 9 and 10, and now this is my first book.

Those were prophetic signs of some of the things I would do as I got older. Well, I am a preacher and Teacher, and I was a DJ on the radio for about 6 months with a great following audience at one time for a gospel station.

I recall when I would go in the neighbourhood and get friends and tell them we are going to act like we are in a service, and I will preach and lay hands on you, but when I lay hands on you, you have to fall backwards because that is what happens when hands are laid on you. They did not understand that, and at that time, neither did I.

Well now when I lay hands on people many fall out under the power of the transfer of the glory of God. Why do people fall out? Is it biblical?

When hands are laid on people there is a powerful transfer of anointings that if received will go from one to the other. There is a ministry called the laying on of hands.

The laying on of hands is also a way of sending folk out into ministry and you can see that in Acts 13. It is a divine act and symbol of the Lord laying hands and setting a person apart for his use.

Hebrews 6:2 mentions the doctrine of the laying on of hands. Moses laid hands on Joshua signifying authority, and one time Joshua was filled with the Spirit of wisdom as a result of Moses laying his hands on him. Ananias laid hands on Paul that he may receive the Holy Spirit. Then we see Pater and John lay hands that some may receive the Holy Spirit, and

Paul told Timothy to stir up the gifts that are in him which were given by the laying on of his hands.

In one place Jesus could do no mighty works due to their faith but he laid his hands and healed a few sick.

Even in Mark 16 it tells us to lay hands on the sick and they shall recover. So the laying on of hands is powerful but be careful when you lay hands and who you lay hands on. Be led by the Spirit of the Lord.

I lay hands on people but it is rarely on the head. I believe that the head is a spiritual opening, because David said thou anointest my head with oil and my cup runneth over.

Jesus would touch a hand, etc., not that you cannot lay hands on people's heads, but I usually do not unless led by the Lord. I believe that the top of the head is an opening for the cup of your spirit, and if it runs over, it also can run out. We must be careful of the run out!

I remember my wife and I visited a ministry and a young novice in ministry prophesied to us, and laid his hands on our heads. I did not stop him because I did not want to kill his spirit knowing that he was only a novice, but suddenly my wife and I both testified to each other that we had a headache immediately thereafter.

Now had he known in the spirit our maturity in the things of God, he would have known not to lay hands on our heads because he had nothing to transfer but a headache!

Then a seasoned Prophet gave a word right afterwards and did not lay hands on us because he recognized who we were in the Lord. I then laid hands on my wife's head and mines and all of a sudden, the headache left. Some things you know as you go, and learn as you go.

From that time on we both agreed that we would not allow anyone to lay hands on our heads unless we knew it was the leading of the Lord and they really had a good impartation, etc.

Many times through my life, ever since I received the Lord as my Lord, I feel the hand of the Lord on top of my head, and a powerful sensation of glory will go through my entire body. It is interesting that it is on the head.

Israel laid hands on Ephraim's head, so laying hands on the head is scriptural. Laying hands also represents responsibility and obligations to the person hands are laid upon. There is an impartation from the one laying hands to the one receiving.

So when hands are laid on a person, the anointing and power is transferred from the one laying hands to the other and your physical body can't take the power of the Holy Spirit so your body gives out and you fall down due to the power that overwhelms your body.

When Jesus said whom seek ye, they all fell out or fell to the ground due to the power. Even when he was resurrected, the soldiers fell as dead men, due to the overwhelming power of God! So going out in the spirit or falling as dead is biblical.

There are many other references to the laying on of hands in scripture but we won't keep talking about that now.

There are of course so many more ways that the prophetic is displayed but we will discuss just a few more when we get to the Ministry of the Prophet in the next chapter.

Chapter 7

The Ministry of the Prophet

The ministry of the Prophet is probably one of the most misunderstood of the five ministry gifts mentioned in Article Ephesians Section 4 Subsection 11. The Apostle and the Teacher I am sure is very misunderstood as well.

As a matter of fact, there are many churches that do not even believe Prophets exist, and forget about the existence of Apostles. To add insult to that injury, you never even hear a person called Teacher unless it is for Sunday school.

Although I am an Apostle of Jesus Christ, called and sent by God as an Apostle, I am also a Prophet, and a Teacher. I have been a Pastor as well. As far as an Evangelist, I have never sensed that mantle in my life, although it is needed just as much as all the others.

We must know where the King has placed us or we will not be the effective blessing to the Kingdom of God as we should. If you are just a Teacher, then abide in that, and if you are only an Apostle, then abide in that, and then there are some who hold several ministry gifts, or offices and you will know the primary function in the Holy Spirit.

There are many times when you will know which one is in operation at the time of ministering. However there must be an understanding of what you have been anointed to do, and the mantle you carry as well as the ministry gift you operate in.

Before we get any further, I want to encourage you by saying that it is not based on what a person believes about you, it is based on what God has settled as far as the ministry gift he has called and sent you to operate in.

I knew that when the Lord mantled, anointed, called and sent me to be an Apostle that there would be some that would question that due to ignorance and misunderstanding of what an Apostle is.

I thought that maybe I better not mention that ever and just let the Lord show it to people. However that is also like a Pastor saying I will never mention that I am a Pastor, just let people see it. The Apostle is a ministry gift as well as the Teacher is.

I remember my wife and I going to a service and an Apostle that did not know us told me that the word Apostle was written all on top of my head. On another occasion we went to another ministry, and that Apostle called me Apostle.

Then on many occasions men and women of God saw it and said it. I did not have to mention it, but they knew by the Holy Spirit. Then it kept coming prophetically from many others.

Then my wife and I visited Bishop Bobby Henderson's ministry, and he had invited Prophet Jean M. Domoraud, who is a mighty Apostle and Prophet of God as well.

He did not know me, but as I held in my heart the Apostolic mantle on my life, he looked at me and called me up and said prophetically "I call you Apostle" and then continued on with a powerful prophetic word. When he prophetically uttered that to me, it sealed it!

So the Lord will allow what is on you to be seen by others who are mature in spirit and even sometimes even the immature. Remember the woman at the well perceived Jesus was a Prophet? So it can be seen and noticed by others.

I remember back in the 80's when I first saw Prophet Brian Mosley; I saw the anointing and the amazing grace of the King on his life in such a powerful way. No one had to tell me that was the man of God to minister that evening, even in the midst of the other preachers around, the glory of God on his life was evident. He would wave his hand up, and out you go under the power of glory and his prophetic utterances was on point. The word he would minister then and even presently now was always rich, revelatory, and very impactful.

I remember I went to a hospital to visit the sick, and after praying for a lady who they said had days to live, the doctors wanted me to pray for another lady who was paralyzed from the waist down. As soon as I walked in the patient's room, she indicated that she perceived I was a man of God, and in return I perceived she had faith to be healed. I told her since she perceived I was a man of God, she will start to feel fire in her feet, and legs. Well to make a long story short, her paralysis left immediately and she got up!

She perceived without me saying a word, and people will know by spirit who you are in the Lord. In 2 Corinthians 4, it talks about how we are to commend ourselves to every man's conscious in the sight of the Lord. One way to look at this is the fact that people can see the grace of the Lord on your life.

We have to make people aware of the King, to cause a repentance to their consciousness or unawareness of the King and his Kingdom, as well as his great benefits.
So, if we do not make them conscious of the consciousness that we have of the Lord in our lives, they will never be conscious of what we are conscious about, and they will never be delivered in their conscious, unless we make them conscious, and if we do not make them conscious, then God has to deal with our conscious about not making them conscious!

I remember my brother Bishop Robert Reed prophesied that the world will see my crown, meaning the glory of the Lord upon me. My brother Apostle Paul Reed prophesied that God will restore me for his Glory. I remember even my sister Minister Cynthia Reed telling me that she just knows that God is going to use me mightily everywhere. However, not just family members, many Prophets and Apostles I did not even know said a lot of the same things. However, it is a blessing when family sees it because Joseph's family did not see it on him beforehand!

As a matter of fact, I remember telling Bishop Willie Robinson when I was under his ministry that I saw Jesus and he commanded me to preach the gospel, and he replied that he already knew God called and sent me, and then indicated he was waiting for me to tell him. One amazing thing about when the Lord appeared to me was that the Lord himself told me that when I tell my Pastor, Bishop Robinson at that time, to tell him I sent you! Amazing that the Lord recognizes those leaders over us that we should have accountability to!

My point is that the glory that the King places on you will be seen and noticed, but let them see his glory, not yours! Never get in the way of his glory although he glorifies us, to God be the Glory.

Wow, even now while writing this book, Prophet Jean Domoraud just text me saying it is a new season for my ministry. My God, my King, this is amazing. The prophetic is just amazing even in its timing. He is such a wonderful man of God!

Let's look at Article Ephesians Section 4 Subsection 8-13. It says *"Wherefore he saith, when he ascended up on high, he led captivity captive, and gave gifts unto men. (Now that he ascended, what is it but that he also descended first into the lower parts of the earth? He that descended is the same also that ascended up far above all heavens, that he might fill all things.) And he gave some, apostles; and some, prophets; and some, evangelists; and some, pastors and teachers; For the perfecting of the saints, for the work of the ministry, for the edifying of the body of Christ: Till we all come in the unity of the faith, and of the knowledge of the Son of God, unto a perfect man, unto the measure of the stature of the fulness of Christ."*

Here we see the three fold purpose of these ministry gifts, for the perfecting of the saints, for the work of the ministry, and for the edifying of the body of Christ.

Perfecting is the Greek word katartismus which means complete furnishing and equipping. These gifts are to equip you and furnish you. The job is not for the ministry gifts to do everything, this is why they train and equip and furnish you so you can do the service of the King in the Kingdom of God.

Working is the Greek word ergon, and implies working, or that which you are occupied in doing. In other words the acts and deeds, we train you in certain areas to bring out your gifting's, callings, etc. The word for edifying is the Greek word oikodome. This really means to build you up for growth and maturity.

The Lord told me although this is what these ministry gifts do, each one has a certain anointing and way that it is done and that is why you have a set of five because they all work differently.

I can say a whole lot on all of the scripture above but I will stick with the points we want to bring out.

These are five ministry gifts that the Lord gave to the Church but we are primarily focusing on the ministry of the Prophet.

However by giving a little information on the other ministry gifts, this will help keep a balance when we get to the Prophet so you can see the distinction of each one although they all have the three fold purpose as mentioned, each ministry gift still works differently.

An Apostle is a sent one by the Lord and when you see the life of Paul who was an Apostle, they were used in all 9 gifts of the Spirit as mentioned in 1 Corinthians 12, mighty works, and miracles were performed, (2 Corinthians 12:12) they are preachers of the gospel (1 Timothy 2:7) as all five of these are, some establish ministries, but there are different kinds of Apostles, or classifications of Apostles.

Apostles also establish different works, and they always will have a strong specific assignment from the Lord. For instance, Paul was an Apostle unto the Gentiles according to 2 Timothy 1:11.

Many Apostles are mantled as Spiritual Fathers or Mothers as well as some Prophets. Let me say that spiritual Fatherhood is not a gender issue; I just wanted to mention that.

Apostles exhort, and comfort, and they are also builders. Many Apostles have seen the Lord, as Paul an Apostle admitted he saw the Lord, not like the other twelve, but he did see the Lord appear to him. Apostles have an extraordinary relationship with the Lord. Many Apostles minister by revelation.

Apostles also function in other areas of the five ministry gifts, such as the Teacher, or Prophet for example. Many have the ability to train leaders and other ministries. However again the Apostle always has an assignment from the Lord and the Apostle focuses on that assignment until it is done and moves to the next assignment as the Lord gives him.

So you have Apostles that walked with Christ while he was on earth, you have foundational New Testament Apostles, and you also have the Apostles of today that are used mightily as aforementioned.

By the way, according to Hebrews 3:1, Jesus was an Apostle!

Apostles do not have the authority to run someone's local ministry, that job is only for the Pastors of that local ministry, so Apostles must understand to stay in their respective places.

The Evangelist has a specific calling, sending and equipping to specifically motivate folk over to the Lord. Evangelist means bringer of good tidings or news. Evangelists are anointed with winning souls to Christ. They do not really try to preach deep truths, although they can, but their anointing is for soul wining.

In Acts 8:5, Philip, the Evangelist, (Acts 21:8) had a heart burning message to let people know about the Lord. There are usually many miracles as well as healings with the Evangelist ministry and this is seen with Philip in Acts 8.

As a matter of fact, Philip preached the gospel of the Kingdom of God in Acts 8, and we see the Evangelist has a word that brings faith, because when he preached many believed and were baptized. Oh how I love the gospel of the Kingdom of God message, for it is the only message Jesus preached and authorized.

Let me say that all preachers have a heart for winning the lost to Christ but the Evangelist has a specific enablement, and anointing to minister in a way that wins souls to Christ.

I remember a certain Evangelist would preach on the trains and have such an anointing for it and the people's hearts were focused on his message. I was not anointed like he was, although I could have ministered on the train too but I would not have been as effective as he was.

Philip was an effective Evangelist but not with getting people filled with the Holy Spirit, if so the Apostles that heard about the word he was ministering would not have had to call on Peter and John.

Let's look at this in scripture. *"But when they believed Philip preaching the things concerning the kingdom of God, and the name of Jesus Christ, they were baptized, both men and women Then Simon himself believed also: and when he was baptized, he continued with Philip, and wondered, beholding the miracles and signs which were done, Now when the apostles which were at Jerusalem heard that Samaria had received the word of God, they sent unto them Peter and John Who, when they were come down, prayed for them, that they might receive the Holy Ghost (For as yet he was fallen upon none of them: only they were baptized in the name of the Lord Jesus Then laid they their hands on them, and they received the Holy Ghost."* So this demonstrates that the Evangelist stayed in his lane.

The Pastor is the only shepherd over the flock, or manager of the local assembly. Some call them the undershepherds since Jesus is the Chief Shepherd.

They are the ones that exercise care, love, provide protection, and a lot of Pastors are also Teachers, although a Teacher is still not necessarily a Pastor. Jesus had compassion because some did not have shepherds and were like sheep gone astray. We need Pastors and every sheep needs a place to graze!

The shepherd, and yes there were female shepherdess as well, would have complete responsibility and oversight of the flock and they are stationary like Paul was in his own hired house for a couple of years while operating as a Pastor at that time, preaching the gospel of the Kingdom of God.

Pastors should not think that they are not qualified unless they have 1,000 people in their committed congregation; God will equip you to handle what he has called you to do. Being a Pastor is a lot of work. My wife one time when ministering mentioned that there are 32 types of sheep so that indicates that no sheep are the same.

A Pastor has to counsel, advise, pray, nurture, build, minister, and the list goes on. The Pastor, in my opinion, is the most important of the five because they stay and maintain their posts because everyone needs a Pastor.

The Pastor needs a Pastor or a spiritual Father. Paul said we have many instructors which actually means boy leaders but very few Fathers. Even the Apostles submitted to one another, Paul submitted himself to Peter as he hung out with him for 15 days, and then Paul stood in Peters face once since Peter was to be blamed, showing Peter submitted to Paul as well.

It is amazing that in many ministries the Pastor is submitted to the Deacons, or the board. The Lord anointed the Pastor and the anointing flows down. You cannot flow up! The Pastor is the visionary for the house, not the Deacon or the board, or someone that is older in age. We must do all things decently and in order.

The anointing to oversee the local ministry is not on the Deacon or the board, it is on the Pastor. You cannot operate in an area you are not called and appointed to do so in.

You cannot put a person on the keyboard to play and they do not have the ability to do so, they would just sit there. We have in churches many who are not called to be a Pastor over the congregation but trying to be the Pastor but in reality like the person who is not a keyboard player, they are just sitting there.

Pastors feed the flock with knowledge and therefore we are to be faithful to the ministry we believe we are assigned to.

The Teacher is not the Sunday school teacher. The Teacher is the one who has been called and sent to teach the word with revelation. Teachers are so needed to bring the body into a supernatural revelation that the Holy Spirit gives the Teacher.

They have a supernatural ability to revelate the word of God in such a way that many times you would of read the same scriptures a thousand times and they come along and bring such revelatory insight that you did not even see before.

I believe with all of my heart that this is why the enemy tries to smother this one because again you never hear Teacher so and so, but you will hear of the other four ministry gifts.

I will never forget in my early ministry, I was in the pulpit hooping the word, and yelling as well as hollering it out in my proclamation of the Word. Then while I was ministering, I felt the mantle of the Holy Spirit come upon me and revelation filled my spirit and I started teaching in such a way, and the people admitted that they were highly blessed due to the revelation of the Word. I was then anointed and mantled as a Teacher in the year 1993 and ever since then, there have been revelations from the Lord that flow out of me.

The Teachers gift is so unique because it flows with so much revelation and it causes such recalibration of the mindset.

As a Teacher, the most powerful things you will ever say are usually away from your notes. There is divine revelation that just comes away from notes.

The teaching ministry is beautiful flowing ministry and it does not mean boring flat walk and talk. It is actually very exciting when you revelate the word and people are receiving it.

Teaching is just like a river flow, once in that vein it keeps on flowing. In Acts 3:1, it mentions certain Teachers and as they ministered and fasted, the Holy Spirit sent them forth. Many Teachers move throughout the body teaching the word.

Many people still think that this is referring to Sunday school teachers; well they did not even have Sunday school in biblical days. Sunday school started around the 17th and 18th centuries!

Keep in mind that the Teacher teaches by a divine anointing, not by Bible College studies, or because one may have a degree. Colleges and Bible schools do not make preachers. I have heard many ask what school a person goes to so they can become a preacher. The answer is no school can make you a preacher, Apostle, Prophet, Evangelist, Pastor, Teacher, or a minister of the gospel. It is a divine calling and appointment by the Lord, not man.

Man can affirm it; because even Jesus was affirmed by John when John said behold the Lamb. Jesus was then introduced by John. In Acts 13 they laid hands on them and sent them. However, many went and were never sent!

"A Went ministry is not a Sent ministry. You do not send yourself, because if you do you are not equipped or qualified!"

With none of these ministry gifts do you just wake up and say I am an Apostle, it is a gift from the Lord to the church, and God always equips whom he calls and sends. All of these ministry gifts require great responsibilities.

We must understand again that you do not send yourself, that is a went ministry, and a went ministry is not a sent ministry. You do not send yourself, because if you do, you are not truly equipped or qualified.

School is good for further learning, but school cannot call and send you to do the work of the five ministry gifts. Remember he, the Lord gives these gifts. The anointing will always evidence the call.

Now the Prophets ministry is the one that we really want to concentrate on but it is good to understand the others in part so we can see the distinguishing elements of the Prophet.

Let me stress again that there are Prophets today, and I am a witness that Prophets exist because I have been a Prophet since 1996 myself. I will never forget that I never told anyone at the time I was a Prophet, and walked in a church, sat in the back, the Pastor did not know me, and he said to me "Hey bless you Prophet, I want you to minister this Sunday." I sat up wondering how he knew I was a Prophet.

People will surely see the prophetic mantle and grace on your life and then eventually experience it as you go forth.

We must understand that if there are no Prophets, then the other four do not exist either. Prophets did not stop in biblical days, neither did the Pastor.

The Prophet is one who is called, appointed and anointed by God to speak the mind of God many times by a sudden strong urge by the Spirit of the Lord. A Prophet will carry revelatory gifts of the Spirit in their lives such as the gift of prophecy, the word of wisdom, the word of knowledge, the gift of tongues and the interpretation of tongues. These gifts are clearly seen in the life of the Prophet or Prophetess.

As a matter of fact, many Prophets sometimes move in all the gifts of the Spirit, but the ones I mentioned are usually pretty dominant along with the gift of discerning of spirits. Paul knew the lady that called herself exalting their ministry was demonically influenced, so he just casted the devil out. As a Prophet he knew this by the discerning of spirits.

Yes Paul was a Prophet according to Acts 13:1 as he was noted as a Teacher and Prophet.

Prophets are not spooky, they just have a peculiar anointing on their lives, and they do not just speak judgment is coming on a ministry as many think. Prophets preach the word of God and they minister how the Lord gives it to them to minister.

A Prophet carries a mantle to pass an anointing in ministry such as Elijah passed his anointing onto Elisha. Prophets do prophesy but just because a person prophecies that does not make them a Prophet. A person with the gift of prophecy can prophesy but a Prophet has a stronger anointing in that area because a Prophet gets the mind of God in a deeper way.

As a matter of fact, God does nothing unless he reveals his secrets to the Prophet, his servant. So in other words, there are moves of God that are revealed to the Prophet by God and the Prophet of God can reveal these moves of God to the people of God if the Lord wills it.

God has secret council meetings in heaven. Remember he is a King and he is a Judge. In Article Amos Section 3 Subsection 3 it says *"Surely the Lord GOD will do nothing, but he revealeth his secret unto his servants the prophets."*

The Hebrew word "secret" here is "cowd" which actually means council and assembly.

Let's look at several passages to bring out my point. Psalm 82:1 says *"God standeth in the congregation of the mighty; he judgeth among the gods."* Then Job 15:8 says *"Hast thou heard the secret of God? and dost thou restrain wisdom to thyself?"*

Let's look at a few more scriptures. In Genesis 1:26, he said let us make man. Then in Job 2:1 he talked about when the sons of God came to present themselves before the Lord. Even Jeremiah 23:18 says *"For who hath stood in the counsel of the LORD, and hath perceived and heard his word? Who hath marked his word, and heard it?"* So there are heavenly meetings, and God can and does reveal many things to Prophets.

Now you may say that the Bible says the secret of the Lord is with them that fear him, and yes it is, but for the Prophet it is talking about the actions and plans of God.

This is why so many Prophets can speak from the side you have not arrived to yet because they have been privy to Gods plans for your life in some cases.

The Bible declares these secret council meetings by what Prophet Micaiah saw. King Jeshosophat was receiving words from Prophets telling him go forth into battle, so he sent for the Prophet Micaiah to see what he would say, although he would say that this Prophet never has anything favourable to say to me, but this Prophet saw the secret council of God.

The King and Judge does have council meetings in heaven, and if the Church would learn about the Judge side of God, and the King side of God, and the Lord side of God, and the Father side of God. The approaches will match the results!

Let's look at Article 1 Kings Section 22 Subsections 17-22, it says *"And he said, I saw all Israel scattered upon the hills, as sheep that have not a shepherd: and the LORD said, These have no master: let them return every man to his house in peace. And the king of Israel said unto Jehoshaphat, Did I not tell thee that he would prophesy no good concerning me, but evil? And he said, Hear thou therefore the word of the LORD: I saw the LORD sitting on his throne, and all the host of heaven standing by him on his right hand and on his left. And the LORD said, Who shall persuade Ahab, that he may go up and fall at Ramothgilead? And one said on this manner, and another said on that manner. And there came forth a spirit, and stood before the LORD, and said, I will persuade him. And the LORD said unto him, Wherewith? And he said, I will go forth, and I will be a lying spirit in the mouth of all his prophets. And he said, Thou shalt persuade him, and prevail also: go forth, and do so."*

All the host of heaven was standing on the Kings left and right side as the King asked a question in the heavenly meeting. Different ones answered, and then here comes forth a spirit indicating that he would persuade Ahab.

Prophets can speak a word and change the course of things. In 1 Samuel 3:19, we see that the Lord would not allow one word the Prophet Samuel would speak to fall to the ground or fail.

Remember Prophet Elisha cursed the 42 children that said "go up baldhead" and two she bears mauled all of them because the Prophet proclaimed it? God backs up Prophets in peculiar ways.

Do you see the trust and honor of God's Prophet? It is to the point where in essence if you say it, I will bring it to pass! Prophets are so very uniquely used by the Lord and so many people want to be Prophets and move in lanes that the Lord has not called them to move or be in.

I remember the Lord speaking to me through a Prophet and told me that this is a season where nothing I speak shall fail or fall to the ground. I knew it was the Lord and I started to speak some things and everything I spoke happened and some I am still waiting for them to materialize.

God honors what a Prophet speaks and sometimes a Prophet does not have to even say the Lord said, because a Prophet can speak a word and God will honor it just because.

Prophets are anointed in such a peculiar way and most are not received in their own country just like Prophet Jesus said of himself. As a matter of fact, many times Prophets are not even received by fellow Prophets or the Church in general due to jealousy, misunderstandings, ignorance, past experiences, etc.

The way a Prophet moves is so very peculiar because God has Prophets say and do many things that may not be agreeable to many. I remember a mother once brought her little girl up in a prayer line confessing to me that she had an abnormal heart murmur. The Lord then impressed in my spirit, to place my finger inside a cup of water, stir it, and tell the girl to drink it.

Now I had just ministered, and I had not stopped to wash my hands, so this sounds a little off, but she went to the doctors the next day and came back with a testimony, after running tests, the murmur was totally gone. Praise the Lord for his mighty move, but imagine if I thought this was a crazy move and this was not the Lord leading me, then her healing would not have taken place.

Prophets are used in such mighty ways. For instance, Jesus was not the first Prophet to cause a miracle of everybody eating from a little source. The word of God clearly indicates the 5 loaves and two fish were for a little boy. So you have a little boy's lunch enough for him. This is key to notice because I once said many years ago that the boy's mother never knew she was really packing for over 5,000 people. Never think the little you have is not enough for the many that will show up!

However there was a Prophet named Elisha who in Article 2 Kings Section 4 (see I am getting you to flow with these Sections and Subsections and then back to what we are used to, and then back again, to get you used to this way for the Constitution of Heaven) that had a company of Prophets and they needed to eat.

One of the sons of the Prophet Elisha found some wild vines and did not know what kind of gourds, or fruit it was and placed it in the pot, and others noticed that death was in the pot, in other words this wild stuff will kill us if we eat it.

Elisha then put meal in it and they ate it and no one suffered from it. Wow, a miracle in the meal! Then someone brought 20 loaves of barley bread, and the Prophet said give it to the men to eat. One of the sons responded by inquiring of the Prophet how a 100 men would eat 20 loaves of the bread. I must say mathematically that would not add up, so good question. The Prophet said the Lord said they would eat, and there would be some left over, and sure enough that was the case!

God uses Prophets to produce the miraculous in mighty ways. It is amazing to me how the Lord thinks verses how we do but after all, he is who he is! Let's now take a look at one more miraculous peculiar event from the hands of a Prophet.

The Prophet Elijah told the woman who was about to eat with her son and die, to give him a piece of cake first. Now that sounds crazy that you would want to eat first of the portion that was for a mother and her son before they die, but he understood the principle of reciprocation.

"The church is greedy and stingy simultaneously. We want the miracle of a Prophet for us, but not the release to the Prophet from us!"

Wow, that is a tough statement, but yet very true. Giving to a Prophet produces miracles on your behalf and until the Church understands seedtime and harvest, the ministry of reciprocation, giving and receiving, we will be stumped in many areas. It is amazing that the church is greedy and stingy simultaneously. We want the miracle of a Prophet for us, but not the release to the Prophet from us! We will get into more of this in chapter nine.

Prophets are used mightily in the miraculous, like the floating ax that was drowning for it was borrowed as mentioned in 2 Kings 6. All the Prophet did was cut down a stick and threw it in the water and the ax swam, or floated! It was borrowed, so the Prophet got him out of debt!

They wanted to build a place there as a school of the Prophets because they were called the sons of the Prophets. This is why the ministry of the Prophet must be taught, and explained. It is fine to teach on the prophetic because there is such a wrong perspective on it.

In Article Kings Section 4 Subsection 38, the sons of the Prophets were sitting in front of the Prophet Elisha. Well they were not just looking at him; obviously he would have been instructing and teaching them.

We see a school of the Prophets signified also in 1 Samuel 19:20 where it says *"And Saul sent messengers to take David: and when they saw the company of the prophets prophesying, and Samuel standing as appointed over them, the Spirit of God was upon the messengers of Saul, and they also prophesied."*

Notice the Prophet Samuel was standing appointed over them and the amazing part is as you read, on all three occasions messengers prophesied, and king Saul himself joined the prophecy party and prophesied. Prophecy turns you into another man!

We must also realize the fact that certain Prophets have certain specific roles in the Kingdom of God. Some Old Testament Prophets spoke whenever Israel broke their side of the covenant agreement. Then Some Kings would go to the Prophets before they went to war. Some Prophets were for the governmental nations, and the Lord will give opportunities for Prophets to speak to Presidents, Kings, and the like.

Now we must see that the ministry of the Prophet continued from the Old Testament Covenant into the New Testament covenant because again remember that Jesus was a Prophet, also Agabus was a Prophet, Paul was a Prophet, Anna was a Prophetess, and some of you reading this book are Prophets, and so I must state again the ministry of the Prophet has not stopped!

The church today needs to be challenged and confronted by Prophets to cause realignment to the focus of the Kingdom of God.

Prophets pray a lot because they must be in the presence of God to receive his word. Therefore they are anointed to pray. Jesus would pray for many hours because he would pray a great while before day and then work miracles in minutes.

It is amazing that the only thing the disciples asked Jesus to teach them was how to pray! They noticed the miracles of this Prophet were usually after he prayed!

Prophets go through, and in case I did not say this, Prophets go through. When I say go through, many people say they want this anointing on this person, or the same anointing on that person, but Prophets go through tough, rough times that I am convinced that many others do not face like Prophets do.

If you do not think Prophets go through, then read these next verses from Article Hebrews Section 11 Subsections 32-38. It says *"And what shall I more say? for the time would fail me to tell of Gedeon, and of Barak, and of Samson, and of Jephthae; of David also, and Samuel, and of the prophets: Who through faith subdued kingdoms, wrought righteousness, obtained promises, stopped the mouths of lions. Quenched the violence of fire, escaped the edge of the sword, out of weakness were made strong, waxed valiant in fight, turned to flight the armies of the aliens. Women received their dead raised to life again: and others were tortured, not accepting deliverance; that they might obtain a better resurrection And others had trial of cruel mockings and scourgings, yea, moreover of bonds and imprisonment They were stoned, they were sawn asunder, were tempted, were slain with the sword they wandered about in sheepskins and goatskins; being destitute, afflicted, tormented; (Of whom the world was not worthy:) they wandered in deserts, and in mountains, and in dens and caves of the earth."*

Look at this list, some were tortured, some experienced cruel mockings and scourgings, bonds and imprisonments, stoned, sawn apart, killed by swords, afflicted, and so much more. Look at what Jesus went through, and Paul, and the list goes on. Prophets are usually not with the crowd, and have very few real friends.

Prophets face situations and circumstances due to their unique calling and stand for the Lord. There is no Prophet that I know of personally who has not experienced mighty trials in one way or another that was uniquely different from a person who is not a Prophet.

The Prophet is questioned concerning his ways of ministry due to it not fitting other people's theologies, and traditions. It is because a true Prophet follows God, and Gods ways are not always the ways of people. Jesus spit in someone's eye, but try that today.

I remember a person had pains in their stomach and the Lord had me to punch them in their stomach, and the pain left immediately. Lord help me, that was not an easy instruction to follow, but the obedience brought a mighty result.

The Prophets ministry suffers jealousy from many others due to the extraordinary way the Lord uses Prophets. It is very unfortunate that this ministry is idolized by many as well and should never be idolized by the Prophet himself or others.

Prophets are often ridiculed, talked against and many are considered false before you realize their realness. A Prophet should never be called a false Prophet unless they live a total life of hypocrisy, just like someone who is saved should never be called a false or fake saint unless they are living the life of hypocrisy as well.

We must realize the fact that if anyone who is saved, whether a minister or not, confesses their sins to the Lord, he is faithful and just to forgive them their sins and cleanse them from all unrighteousness according to 1 John 1:9.

This means that confessed sin is now null and void in the eyes of the Lord.

The enemy uses people to talk against the Prophet because if you believe the Prophet you will prosper so if he can mess up their names, it can cause people not to prosper, but God knows how to fix that too. You can't believe all you hear.

Many times we forget all of the sins we have personally done that no one may not know about but we are so quick to judge others based on misinterpretations, or what people say, and the like. We must stop fighting one another, and keep our own selves in check.

Many times when being attacked, silence is the best thing because if two people are fighting in the mud you cannot tell who is winning anyway. Keep silent and let God fight the battle.

There are times that Prophets will go through something that the people will go through before they will even go through it. This is a deep part many do not understand. Why so much happens to the Prophet? Many times it is the preparation of what will happen in your life.

Jeremiah was in captivity before the people were in captivity, and today many Prophets go through before people do, and the ones that do not understand will say they must have done something to deserve this.

Many times Prophets will not even be understood or even accepted by their own family members, because many times Prophets are not involved in things others are involved in.

The Prophet is faced with many things that seem to be contradictory of even what God has said to them. For instance, God tells the Prophet Elijah to go to a widow woman that he commanded to feed him, and when he gets there, she does not even have enough food for herself and her son!

Have you ever been given a word, and the circumstance does not seem to relate to the word at all, yet you know it was God that spoke it? We must hold on to the words of the Lord no matter what it looks like.

The Prophet shows a lot of love although many do nothing but criticize and bash while ministering without showing the love of the Father. God comes against sin, and yet he loves.

Sometimes we choose what to minister based on thinking the job of a Prophet is to only come down hard on you but that is a realization of misunderstanding the ministry gift of the Prophet. If we are going to mention sin, let us also mention how to get out of it. Prophets are to show the love of the King.

It is amazing how God told Prophet Hosea to marry a wife of whoredom and love her even though she had to be bought back from another man. God was using this Prophet to show how God felt and how God loves. Prophets feel the heart of God on many occasions.

Prophets go through for refining, and the Lord does refine Prophets in the most unique ways so they can come out and forth as pure gold! A Prophet is dealt with by God in many ways so they can have what God intends for them to have and to be.

It costs to be a Prophet in ways that many do not want, but along with the calling and the sending of the Prophet, comes the sufferings that go with that ministry gift.

Prophets need not be concerned about many engagements to minister at ministries, or wherever. There is timing for everything and you may think you are ready to go all over the world, but know that God will make opportunity for you at the right time.

There may be more pruning in your life that needs to take place, or you may need to face a few more things that will make you strong. You may need more time for development. Having a Lamborghini at age five is nice, but it does you no good until the proper time.

Now with that in mind you may be thinking this is right based on the scripture that says your gift will make room for you, but please let us not use that scripture for this context.

Let me give you a quick reason why we do not want to use that scripture about your gift will make room for you because it is not in the context of gifts as we think. You may be shocked, but here we go. Let us briefly look at that scripture. It says in Article Proverbs Section 18 Subsection 16 *"A man's gift maketh room for him, and bringeth him before great men."*

The word "gift" in the Hebrew is "mattan" and it actually means offering! Uh oh! You mean to tell me that gift here did not mean talents or anointing? That is correct. It has nothing to do with your talents of singing, poetry, etcetera, it is referring to offerings.

How do your offerings make room for you? Well the word room here refers to growth, so your offerings makes growth for you and brings you before great men of importance.

In biblical cultural times, in the Middle East, they would bring many gifts so they could be heard by the individual they were bringing gifts to. Especially going before a king, you could not go before a king without a gift to bring because this would not be in order or acceptable.

This is why Kingdom etiquette is so important so we can even know how to approach our King. Proverbs is a good book on Kingdom etiquette.

The queen of Sheba brought gold to king Solomon because she heard of his wisdom, and he answered all of her questions which had to take time, and his wisdom took her breath away, but her gifts made that kind of room for her, because there were many who came before Solomon, but notice he answered all her questions which shows it not only made room for her before someone great but it also made time for her in front of someone great.

Everyone that wanted his wisdom brought gifts to him. On top of that he gave her everything she desired, answered her questions and then gave her of his royal bounty!

It is amazing that she gave and received as well from a great man, a king. When we give offerings we give to the King!
Jacob sent gifts to Esau and it brought him before God who wrestled with him all night. He even said I will appease Esau with these gifts and perhaps he will see my face.

The King of Kings gave his son as a gift and it made room for the King to have more kings and sons. Your gift makes or causes you to be brought before great men. This is a favor on your gift giving. I remember one time I gave and someone immediately sowed in my life before I even got to my seat!

I believe your gift brings you favor and opportunities before great men and then in return you will leave these great men with an impartation far worth the giving. This is one reason that the enemy hates when people give to Prophets, because they receive great things back.

We wonder when we give to the Prophet what is the Prophets reward. I would like to share that with you while we are on the gift giving.

Let us look at the scripture that refers to the Prophets reward. Matthew 10:41-42 says *"He that receiveth a prophet in the name of a prophet shall receive a prophet's reward; and he that receiveth a righteous man in the name of a righteous man shall receive a righteous man's reward. And whosoever shall give to drink unto one of these little ones a cup of cold water only in the name of a disciple, verily I say unto you, he shall in no wise lose his reward."*

It talks of the rewards for the Prophet, the righteous man and the little ones as Jesus refers to them. Just for time sake, one of the rewards for the righteous is the receiving of what they believed, and of course eternal life. Abraham believed and it was counted unto him for righteousness. Just hungering for righteousness fills you.

The little ones here are referring as a term of endearment to his children. Remember when Jesus talked about offending one of his little ones that believe in him, that it is better to be casted and drowned into the depths of the sea?

Well the reward of believers is eternal life as well as what the Word promises. What a reward! I tell you the King is worthy of all of our praises, but let's get on with some more information because I love to praise him!

The reward of the Prophet is interesting and great as well. One of the Prophets rewards is the fulfilment of what the Prophet has spoken which is also based on your belief of that word.

It is important to understand that a reward is something given in response of something done. In the case of the widow woman, she did what the Prophet told her and gave to him first, and then she received a reward of fulfilment her own self.

If you read 2 Kings 4, you will discover something interesting in reference to the Prophets reward. This shunammite woman perceived that Elisha was a man of God, and he asked what she wanted, and she received from the Prophet, and the reward, to make a long story short, was her breakthrough, and the raising of her promised son back from the dead.

The Prophet's reward from this story is understanding that the answers to your desires are manifested!

This all started with giving, and it is important to understand seed sowing, and harvest reciprocation. Staying around the Prophet, gets you a reward, because mantles are passed on, and anointing's are given!

Another point regarding Prophets is the fact that since Prophets see so far ahead, sometimes frustration can come and if accepted can discourage a Prophet because they wait so long for what they see so far ahead.

Many Prophets can also feel what others are dealing with and therefore if they are not careful, they can be seduced by that same spirit even upon themselves.

Speaking of feelings, this is actually another way that God uses Prophets. The prophetic can be displayed through a Prophet by feelings in their physical bodies. A Prophet can suddenly have a headache on the right side of the head but it is the pain someone else feels that may be sitting in the congregation for instance, and when he calls it out, the person responds and is healed.

I remember the time when I kept getting a deafness feeling in my ear, and for three nights straight I kept asking does anyone have an ear problem. On the first two nights no one responded.

Then on the third night of the meeting, a man came forward confessing a deaf ear due to a motorcycle accident. After commanding the ear to be restored and the deaf spirit to come out, I whispered in his ear, and not only did he hear me, his mother came up and whispered and he heard her too. She was amazed, the people were amazed, and we all glorified the King of Kings and Lord of Lords.

My wife on many occasions has felt different feelings in her body of pain in certain areas and without fail, there has always been someone either in the congregation or at another time somewhere else that had the pain in the exact spot, and after she ministers to them, it is gone.

God will use any of your senses to display a prophetic movement. One time my wife smelt gas in the morning, and we had all electricity, but when we got to service, she prophesied to someone that they loved the smell of gas, and they admitted that they really do and prophetically she explained it to them in such detail and they were amazed at the prophetic word.

I have smelt certain smells and just knew it was a certain kind of spirit. I have smelt sickness on people, and knew what to pray for. I have even smelt certain lifestyles in the spirit as crazy as that may sound. It is a certain smell that goes with certain lifestyles and it is always the same smell when a certain lifestyle of a person comes around me without fail.

See in the Spirit, you can smell something and not see it, like you can smell barbecue if you are close, but may not see it, well it works the same in the Spirit.

A Prophet can also have a certain taste in his mouth and know things by that taste.

I will never forget one time in service, there were no windows opened, and I knew the presence of an angel was to my left, and all of a sudden I heard and felt a strong wind blow in my ear. I asked if anyone else heard it, and many on different rows heard, and some only felt it at the same exact time.

I believe it meant that God was opening my spiritual ears with a higher reception of what he is saying and doing. It was so amazing! It actually felt like air was blown through a small cylindrical device, or a straw.

This is why a Prophet has to be so sensitive to the Spirit of the Lord. A Prophet may feel a pain in his finger representing a person has a finger pain. So our sensitivity must grow in the things of God to know how he displays the prophetic.

"The Word of God is not always heard, sometimes it is only manifested!"

We must understand that the Word of God is not always going to be heard, sometimes it is only going to be manifested, and we also must understand that the manifested Word that was not heard still has meaning to it.

So a Prophet has to hear what his fingers are telling him, what his foot is telling him, what his eyes are telling him, what his body is telling him because there can be manifested feelings that must be interpreted and understood as it relates to others.

Many in the church do not believe in praise dancers, or prophetic dancing, but God uses the dancing ministry as a message to him, and a message through the dancers to us.

Prophetic communication cannot be fought when it is God because he has so many different ways of displaying his communication.

Jeremiah put a yoke on his neck to display the communication of the King, so the point is that we must understand that whatever way God uses to display his message is prophetic.

Many times Prophets are pressured to give a prophetic word to different people and should never yield to that pressure. It is a Word from the Lord that must be exercised when God gives it.

However we learn that going through is interesting as well because it builds us, and it causes us to have an experience that can encourage others in such a profound way. When you minister and have not been through much, keep ministering!

Let me say this, do not try to become a Prophet because someone says you look like one, please note that it is a calling and a sending from God.

The Prophet is an ordained mouthpiece for God, speaking suddenly the words of the Lord as the Lord gives him. A Lot of times when ministering, you can tell the shifting of a Prophet from one vein to another.

The Prophet is also involved in judging a prophetic word if it is from the Lord or not per 1 Corinthians 14:29.

Prophets can operate in what is called or termed prophetic presbytery. It is when a group of Prophets can gather and give words from the Lord, and also lay hands and send forth into ministry as well as give an impartation to the recipient.

Let's read 1Timothy 4:14, it says *"Neglect not the gift that is in thee, which was given thee by prophecy, with the laying on of the hands of the presbytery."* The gift was given by prophecy and the laying on of hands by the presbytery.

The Prophet can request of the Lord to open your eyes to see something he sees that you do not see. I am sure you remember the story in 2 Kings 6 where the Prophet prayed that the servant's eyes would be opened. It is amazing that so many angels were there. I believe that the bigger your assignment is, the more angels are around you.

Let me add that if you are a Prophet in a local ministry that has a Pastor, the Prophet is still not the Pastor of that local assembly. This can bring down a lot of unnecessary tension.

There are Pastors that will not make a move unless the Prophet in the local ministry approves it. That is not Kingdom order.

"Sometimes we respect the Prophet more than the one who gives the Prophet the prophecy!"

We must be careful because sometimes we respect the Prophet even more than the one who gives the Prophet the prophecy.

The Prophet is not over a ministry where there is a Pastor, and remember the Pastor is the manager of that house and receives the word of the Lord for that ministry. The Pastor in a local ministry is over the Prophet or anyone else who joins that ministry. They can and should work together to bring the body of Christ into its full maturity, but the Pastor has the say so, period.

I have heard people ask concerning local ministries who the Prophet of the house is, the answer is the Pastor. Although there may be a Prophet in the house, the Prophet is not the voice on the head of that house. The mouth is on the head, not the body! Again, the mouth isn't not on the body, not on the board, or the deacons, but on the visionary of the house!

I want to also add that if you are a married Prophet with a wife who is not in ministry; never put your wife on what I will call a prophetic altar of killings where she has no say so because you are the big headed Prophet. God even told Abraham to listen to his wife because the wife has eyes that a lot of the husbands do not have even if they are Prophets.

Notice God drove the man out the garden, and I believe Eve followed because she knew who to blame because she had the eyes.

I also recommend traveling with your wife when ministering if at all possible. It is good for obvious reasons, and for strength. When I minister, my wife is always watching as well as praying to strengthen me and to ward of any attacks that may try to come by spirit. It is good all around.

If you are a Prophetess and you are married to a husband who is not in ministry, keep in mind there is the ministry of the Prophetess and the wife. Respect your husband. Do not make him feel that since you are the Prophetess you are the leader and he will die if he does not do what you say, and he is the follower as you lead. That is not Kingdom order. So, operate together in a lovely flow of harmony in your marriage. Travel with your husband for the same reasons as mentioned above.

If you're an unmarried Prophet, then stay before the Lord and when you minister out, minister and leave as soon as you can to prevent the unnecessary that can try to tempt or taint you. Simply put, it is not worth it and you do not need on you what is not needed on you. The anointing is good enough for you.

If you are an unmarried Prophetess stay before the Lord and when you minister out do the same thing as mentioned above, leave. The enemy can be very slick and will always bring pride, money, a person, a proposition, and the like and again, it is not even worth it. Now people will accuse you regardless, but just keep walking in the admonition of the Lord, and you will be fine.

This is why the accompaniment of strong folk in ministry is good to be around you so they can support and uphold you.

If you are the spouse of a minister and you are not a minister yourself, always be as supportive and prayerful for that minister as possible. There are times that the married spouse that is not in ministry may not understand some ministerial things, but the married minister should communicate and explain where there is an even understanding.

The minister of the gospel is not married to the Church when he is married or unmarried. If the minister spends all of their time at the Church building, and always with the saints and they are hardly ever with their spouse, or family, then you are showing more interest in Jesus Bride than your own and this will cause unnecessary problems.

He that hath an ear, let him hear what the Spirit says to the Church!

Prophets should pray with their spouse so when there is a word, there is also an agreement because if you get a word as a Prophet that you believe was from God, and the word fails because it was not from God, that spouse may not forget that, and when there is another word you say is from the Lord, you now have a problem.

"A Prophet should not be a babbling voice but a bubbling voice!"

A Prophet must realize that he bubbles forth the words of the Lord to the people and so therefore a Prophet should not be a babbling voice but a bubbling voice. Nabi in the Hebrew is from a root meaning to bubble forth as like a fountain. The Prophet bubbles forth what the Spirit of the Lord places in his belly.

Prophets are used in so many distinctive ways, for instance you hear some Prophets call out people's names and then give them a prophetic word where there is no way they could have known this information unless the Lord reveals it.

Calling a name happened in the Old Testament. The Prophet Isaiah in Isaiah 44 and 45 called out king Cyrus name about 150 years before he was even born and what God will use him for!

It is utterly amazing that the secret things belong to the Lord and when he reveals a name, a number, or any information about you, which also by the way convinces others of the power and omniscience of God, that the first thing we wonder is if the devil told the Prophet. It is the enemy that does not want the Lord to have the credit but thank God that he is big enough to defend himself!

So the prophetic causes us to see behind the world in front of us.

"Prophetic vision sees beyond the visible to the invisible that causes the visible."

Prophets have an anointed eye to see prophetically in such a way. Prophetic vision sees beyond the visible to the invisible that causes the visible. They can see what is not, from what is, into what shall be.

There is even more to say about the Prophet but we are trying to give you just a sense of understanding of the ministry of the Prophet to further clarify things you may not have been clear on.

Prophets not only existed, but still exist today, and are being fought against in so many ways because of the ignorance and misunderstanding as well as the powerful anointing and mantle upon their lives. He that receives the Prophet, receives Jesus, and he who sends him.

Chapter 8

The Giving of a Prophetic Word

Understanding that the giving of a prophetic word is more important than we probably realize because the word comes to the one who is prophesying, and that person must convey that word without adding or tainting it.

It is therefore important to make sure that when we prophesy that we do not mix our own knowledge, theologies, ideas, or fleshly desires into that word that we release.

You may know some facts about a person that may not seem pleasing to the Lord and then the Lord gives a great profound prophetic word to you for them. That is when you must release that word without prejudice.

The Lord does not look on the outward appearance of man but the heart and no one knows them like the King knows them or you for that matter.

We must be careful that we do not interfere with the words of the Lord through us because many can be misguided because they are trusting the prophetic word that you give.

I always advise that we be careful with dates and mates unless you are so beyond sure that the Lord has spoken. I have heard Prophets tell people who will be their wife or husband and it never happened.

I have been prophesied to by Prophets that have given me dates, and they were well known for their accurate prophetic utterances, and some of those dates have passed many moons and even years ago.

This is why when Prophets tell me such and such will happen in ex amount of days or months, I remind them if they are reachable so if it does not happen, they are accountable for that released word.

I will never forget when a notable Prophet told me something was going to happen on a certain date and it did not happen. Since he gave the date, it should have been settled without much effort from me.

I honestly believed what he said would happen on that date, but it did not. I told him about it and he simply replied that he was sorry that he missed it. Now that's humility!

This is why I always say that if while you are flowing and you notice that it is not flowing anymore, stop. Anything other than his flow is your flow!

We prophesy in part and according to our faith, so you must understand that the Lord is not going to give you everything there is to know about something because he is the only one that knows all things.

He will give you a part, or just enough. He speaks because there is a need to speak. If you are not sure, then pray and wait on what you believe the Lord is saying until he has proven that word to you that it is him.

There are times the Lord will give you a word concerning someone and it may not even be for you to tell them then, or at all. It could be that he just wants you to pray to him that he intervenes. God told Daniel to shut the book up until a later time. We have to understand prophetic timing, and not just release everything just because it came to you. Never be a Prophet that feels he or she has to blurt out things all the time. This is where maturity comes to play.

Habakkuk 2 tells us that revelation waits for an appointed time, but at the end it will speak. The way a word is delivered along with the timing of the word can be a blessing or a curse to someone.

I remember one time telling someone prophetically an encouraging word, but the Lord showed me death in their family. It was not time or even a release in my spirit to release what I saw. It could have been more of a curse to them to tell them the death part because that knowledge could have overpowered the encouraging word. That is what I mean when I say a curse to them.

There is timing for prophetic words. The Constitution of Heaven says a word spoken in due season is good, so there is a proper time for prophetic words. I have experienced along with many Prophets that they would prophecy one thing, and not reveal what else the Lord showed them.

Sometimes it is not for people to hear that are around if ministering publicly or it is not the timing for the other part, but we pray on that part. I have spoken in tongues over people after prophesying so the Lord can intercede on what he wants to intercede about through me where no one will know but the Lord.

We must be mature in giving a word of prophecy especially if it is a prophetic word of rebuke in some way. We don't need it shouted over the microphone when it is personal to prevent embarrassment.

If rebuking openly that others may fear, use godly wisdom
You must learn how to communicate the word that the Lord has given to you to give to someone else. He may have you not speak it but write it.

If there is a word from the Lord to you for someone, do not worry, the Lord will make a way for you to get to that person.

A lot of times with the prophetic what you think is the Lord is sometimes you, and what you think is not the Lord sometimes is. A lot of times there is that word that comes quick and leaves, and you are left with the job of catching, holding, and then delivering. It is that word that must be pushed out like a river so it won't be stuck like a lake.

When the Lord gives a word of destruction, or something that will happen to a nation, before blurting that out, pray and ask how it relates to his plan, and what should the hearers do as a result. If not we are just letting people know destruction is coming and that is it.

We need to understand that the prophetic delivery is not a battle of the prophetic. What do I mean? I have seen in services one person prophesy, and then another would interrupt that person and prophesy, and then another with a proud spirit would show he is better and more mature, and the whole thing went from the battle of the prophetic to the battle of the pathetic.

Never try to show yourself, show God. When in a service and you know there is a prophetic word, the King will give opportunity for that word to come forth. One way is in the midst of things, there will be quietness, and that quietness can give you opportunity.

I recall a time I visited a ministry and the Pastor did not know me and brought the microphone to me and told me that I had a word from the Lord. God knows how to give you the opportunity and then by faith you must take it.

I remember the first time I ever prophesied. I was on the organ, and I just knew there was a word from the Lord. The preacher got quiet after giving praise, and then everyone else got quiet as well. I was the only one left still speaking in tongues.

All of a sudden, my spirit came out of my body and I was sitting to the right of my body. I was looking at my body speaking what the Lord was saying and I heard myself saying what I was actually telling myself to say. It was an incredible experience. After the prophetic words, my spirit came back into my body. The word was received and from then on, I never staggered giving the word of God when I knew it was the Lord.

Everyone does not have the same experience or delivery, and this is why God made us all different because he is a God of diversity.

Allow the Holy Spirit to use you in his way. A lot of times God will use your style of character or personality to display his word.

If you are in a service and are not sure if that ministry receives prophetic words to utter in the congregation, then hold it until after service and do all you can to get to the Pastor and let them know what the Lord has given you. It is possible that he will give you opportunity then for all to hear, or another appointed time if received.

If the word is not received, do not worry, you already released it out! Once it is released, then you have completed that assignment.

Sometimes with a prophetic word, we may seem like it is not completed, and that is when we must realize that word or revelation was all you got. I have been pulled on to minister in prophetic presbytery and I would say only what he gave me, sometimes it may be three sentences, and I would say, that is all I have. There is nothing wrong with saying that.

Sometimes we think we must prophecy to the entire congregation, and speak 20 minutes to each person. If you do, you probably will not be invited back. Do not try to impress people, let the word of God flow through you, and out of you, and be sensitive to the Spirit of the Lord and the people.

Remember that what was not finished to you in that short time could be complete for the person that heard and received the word. You do not have to add for their satisfaction; just deliver for the Kings satisfaction.

It is like reading a letter to someone, and at the end, you keep going adding your own words, then you actually are now lying, and showing misrepresentation! This causes a seed of lies to be engrafted into the recipient through their ears and it grows as an artificial birthing. You have two canals, an ear canal as well as a birth canal, and what you hear you birth!

Then we have emotional wombs, mental wombs, spiritual wombs, and the list goes on. Be careful what you release, because there will be a birthday for the recipient.

Sometimes you may see a picture of something while prophesying that you do not understand yourself, it is ok to tell the person what you see and ask if it means anything to them. If it does, then praise God, and if it doesn't, then praise God, move on to the next thing. This is why delivery is important. You are just saying what you see that's all.

Remember God is Spirit, and a lot of things he says or shows us may not make sense to the mind at all because the mind is trying to relate to our born again spirits anyway, and this is why the mind has to constantly be in the process of renewal and recalibration.

When giving a word to someone in a service, sometimes the recipient is speaking in tongues at the same time, or praising God at the same time, or even praying at the same time. When I am giving a word to someone and they are doing all of that at the same time, I ask them to be quiet politely by saying "listen, I want you to hear and get this word".

It is fine to ask them to listen and hear the word, because if not, what would be the purpose of continuing a word that is not heard?

Besides it is rude if God is talking to you, and you are talking to him at the same time. Let one speak, and then the other.

See, Paul said prophesy one by one so that we may all learn, so teaching the prophetic is biblical and needed.

Never ever be offended if a Pastor or someone of maturity in ministry lets you know that the word that you gave was off, wrong, etc. Remember a Pastor usually knows his flock pretty well especially if it is a smaller ministry. However discuss it with the Pastor to get the full clarity, and possibly for you to give it as well if it was not missed. Misunderstandings and perspectives can come into play in the prophetic world.

Know also that you do not have to lay hands on people just to prophesy, get the word out, not the hand out.

There may be times when the Lord will give you three words to start off with, that is when you must continue by faith.

Notice not three words only that would be a completion, I am referring to when you know in your spirit that there is more to say, then start with those words and like a river with your faith it will continue to flow.

Many times I would see like a glow over someone and for me it is an indicator that the Lord has a word for that person. Most of the times I have no idea what that word is until they come up before me, and then it flows out of me to them, and in them.

Many times I have seen people prophesy for ten seconds and then speak in tongues for two minutes, and then back with prophecy, and then go back in tongues for a long time. I suggest that you get as much of the completion of that word as possible so it does not bring confusion where they are getting a part they understand, and then hearing in tongues what they do not understand.

It is fine to speak in tongues prior to prophesying when you have not reached the maturity to just flow, but as you grow you will see it will just flow.

Sometimes you may hear someone speak in tongues and it is not prayer as I mentioned before, but a message and you have the interpretation of what was said, then go forth, because tongues plus interpretation of tongues equals prophecy.

When giving a prophetic word, do not allow their expressions on their faces to bother you. Some people look straight in your eyes, some look like they do not agree, but you must know to keep the flow.

There have been times I know it was the Lord and I would get straight faces and found out they were simply shocked by what was revealed. Everyone is different. Just be the deliverer.

At the same time, do not be pulled into them agreeing constantly because you do not want your flesh to step in and pride step in and you feel yes I got it, based off of their response. You must respond to God, and flow from your spirit in his Spirit.

You should live a life of prayer so you can always be in tune with what God is saying as he relates to your spirit.

There may be times that a prophetic word comes out of you in the form of a song. This has happened with me many times when prophesying. Sometimes it will start off in tongues, and then I will interpret in the same melody.

Remember that prophetic words are words of life, quickened words, so do not go by feelings. Sometimes we think during prophecy we are going to feel a certain power from God, or a strong anointing. This does not happen all the time.

I remember when I laid hands on someone, and they went out in the Spirit and I felt nothing at all, however I had been fasting for five days and this was the fifth day.

Usually I would feel a flow out of my belly into my arms and out of my hands but this time absolutely nothing, yet the release was there and it was mightily effective.

The Lord taught me not to rely on the feelings, rely on his word, Spirit, and faith. So when you prophesy, do not rely on a feeling, rely on his Spirit, if not, we will get to have feeling faith, and not word faith.

Sometimes there is just a knowing in your spirit, then speak what you know prophetically. Don't expect to hear verbal words in your ears; this is why chapter 6 is so important.

There may be a time you are led by the Spirit of God to just pray prophetically for the person. When I say pray prophetically, I am saying to pray as you are led to pray by the Lord.

Let me add this, do not let someone who is trying to get your attention for a prophecy to pull you in to give one, people do this, just move on and be led by the Lord.

There are times, if it has not happened yet, that you will feel the weight of people, or weight in the service, or in the atmosphere. You must discern if this is this the weight of the people or witchcraft attack, or some form of demonic attack against the prophetic.

I have seen people get physically attacked during prophetic services. All of a sudden pains in their legs, or sharp stomach pains, etc. This is a distraction to draw people away from the prophetic release, because the enemy hates when God speaks.

If you are the one with the microphone and in charge of the flowing, do not panic, for this will bring confusion, stay in the flow of the Spirit. Sometimes people will just get up, run and pray for that person, and if it is orderly then that is fine too, but keep the flow in order. Some people do not need to go and lay hands and pray for the person that is attacked. This can give opportunity for the witch to run over there and impart as well in the mix.

The enemy is a smooth operator and he loves to mix in the crowd and blend, and this is why you should live a fasted praying life. Jesus said this kind goes out by fasting and prayer.

Jesus never said if you fast, he said when you fast. Fasting moves you closer to God because you are giving up what the flesh wants and God honors that.

One of man's greatest appetites is food, so you are turning over this appetite for the appetite of being closer to God.

Fasting is not dieting; it is turning down your plate for spiritual reasons. Fasting shows self-denial, and affliction of the soul, and it increases the power of God in your life. I know this personally as a fact!

Fasting allows your spirit to become uncluttered and you become more sensitive to the things of God, and in ministry, and in the prophetic flow fasting and prayer is needed.

However, in the case of any attack during the prophetic flow, one of the best things to do is to bring the people into praise like never before.

God inhabits the praise of his people Israel, but it includes us too because we have been grafted in. This invites the presence of the Lord in a mightier way when we are on one accord in praise.

The Lord showed me that during a loud corporate praise, it drowns out the enemies commands to his cohorts because the praise is so loud, their communication is disrupted.

Let the musicians play under the anointing during this praise because as the musicians play the prophetic is released.

Isaiah 61:3 is a powerful key verse that says *"To appoint unto them that mourn in Zion, to give unto them beauty for ashes, the oil of joy for mourning, the garment of praise for the spirit of heaviness; that they might be called trees of righteousness, the planting of the LORD, that he might be glorified."*

Praise will cloak you with his Glory! What demon can stay then? The demons got to go dot org!

So do not fear, because fear is a spirit, just flow in praise, and watch the King move mightily, and trouble the trouble!

Know that prophetically God speaks what we need to know, not necessarily what we want to know, and the recipient needs to understand this as well.

To prophesy accurately, we must understand some of the ways God speaks as related in the different prophetic displays we discussed.

Instead of getting in the flesh, allow the word to become flesh. In other words be consumed by the Spirit of the Lord and flow in the Spirit.

Remember to fast, pray, and stay in the word of God! This will help increase the realization of the awareness of the Lord. You should surround yourself by Prophets that you know are Prophets in the Lord.

I just believe as you are reading this book the Lord will lead you even farther into the moves of the prophetic.

To help a little in the prophetic before releasing a word that you believe the Lord has given to you to release, here is a list of questions that you can ask yourself to help increase the effectiveness of giving a prophetic word.

A Few Prophetic Questions

Do I sense an urgency of release to give this word?

Is this word edifying, encouraging and will it build?

Does this word agree with the Word of God?

Do I feel pressured to give this word by people because other Prophets are around?

Is there clear opportunity for me to give this word?

Is there an anointing for the word?

Is the word cloudy or clear for release?

How did the word come to you?

Am I persuaded by the Spirit of the Lord?

Is this word sticking in my spirit?

Answering these questions will help in guiding the prophetic word you believe God has placed in you.

Chapter 9

The Receiving of a Prophetic Word

Understanding the receiving of a prophetic word is so vital to the recipient, so we will share just a little to get you on the path to receive correctly with an understanding.

We must understand that it is fine to judge a prophetic word, not the Prophet, but the Word from the Prophet or whoever is prophesying.

Let me preface by saying every word may not necessarily agree with your spirit as in the case of Peter betraying Christ. There is no evidence that Peter agreed with that prophetic word, but it came to pass.

There are times, and in many occasions where the word will agree with your spirit, and then there are times when God is confirming, reminding you, or simply instructing you, but all prophecy will edify you.

In 1 Thessalonians 5:20, it tells us not to despise prophecy. So to hear from the Lord do not have yourself in a position where you have prejudged prematurely before the word even comes, and do not let no one convince you that the Lord does not speak.

You must understand that everyone can prophesy, and it may come from the least expected person. Now since a donkey can prophesy, do not be surprised if your pet speaks a word.

If you close off how the Lord can speak, then you will miss the opportunity for the Lord to speak, so be opened to the Lord speaking, period. Balaam prophesied truth and look at his life!

Do not substitute a Prophet for God. God wants to speak to you and can speak to you himself.

Paul tells us to test prophecies and hold to that which is good. So prophetic utterances must be tested, or judged.

It is recommendable that if you receive a word and you are not sure if it is on point; take that word to your Pastor so they can judge it. This will prevent you from going through the unnecessary.

We must judge the word given because many have received instructions prophetically that have caused negative effects on their lives.

When there is a Prophet, the Bible tells us to believe his Prophets and we will prosper. I must stress again to be careful in judging the Prophet, judge the prophetic word.

The person giving the word can still be immature, but yet have a great portion of the word correct. So have an ear to hear.

If we judge a Prophet is false based on a word that was not true, and then another word he gives is true, we will go up and down with judging this Prophet, so we must be mature ourselves in understanding the reception of a prophetic word.

I have prophesied to people and some said I do not know about that, and then later turn around and say, oh yes, I do recall, and that is correct. This is why we must stay open.

When there is a prophetic word given, it encourages your faith in God even the more, because you see his concern for you, and about you.

In judging prophecy it is important to make sure it lines up with edifying, exhortation, and comfort.

Does it lead me into the truth of God's word? Sometimes it can confirm what you know and add a little more to it.

Sometimes with a word given there can be a check in your spirit that it is the Lord. There are times again that God will speak something prophetically that you did not know. He does not have to always speak to you first before a Prophet can speak to you.

Elisha never knew he would go into ministry, Elijah threw the mantle on him, and there is no mention of David knowing he would be a King, Samuel prophesied and anointed him with a postdated anointing and calling, and the list goes on, so do not block the prophetic based on what you already know.

You must war with prophecy by faith. I like 1 Timothy 1:18 where it says *"This charge I commit unto thee, son Timothy, according to the prophecies which went before on thee, that thou by them mightiest war a good warfare; Holding faith, and a good conscience; which some having put away concerning faith have made shipwreck."*

Holding faith is not letting go and believing the prophetic word will happen as told, or hold onto the encouragement of that word regardless of any circumstances that may arise.

Guard the prophetic word and do not allow it to fall to the ground. Speak that word, and meditate on that word, because remember the prophetic is divinely uttered and inspired.

There are times when a prophetic word will seem impossible to come to pass, but remember Sarah thought the same thing and even laughed to herself, but Abraham never staggered at the promises of God.

"Have patience during the prophetic process because a suddenly never comes unless it was preceded by a process."

It is important to have patience during the prophetic process because a suddenly never comes unless it was preceded by a process. The suddenly in Acts 2 was preceded by prayer. The New Testament was preceded by the Old, and the list goes on.

Knowing the fruit of a Prophet is good because a good tree does not bring forth evil fruit. Keep in mind that the Spirit of prophecy is the testimony of Jesus, so it will always glorify the Lord.

The prophetic will never lead you away from God; it will always draw you closer to him. Even when it is a prophetic word of correction, remember he chastens those he loves.

Let me say this as well, I have heard of Prophets who would try to swindle you for money before you get a Prophetic word by saying things like, "If you give me $5,000 dollars the Lord will do such and such." You just been had if the approach was like that. Be aware of these kinds of Prophets.

On the other hand we must understand that the prophetic is released by music, because the word says as the minstrel played Elisha prophesied.

However it is true that a Prophetic word is also released through giving, and the church has a hard time understanding this concept which is biblical.

There are people who sow a seed after getting a prophetic word, but then will say it is the devil if a seed was sown first and then a prophetic word came.

It is one thing to swindle, but it is another thing to sow. There is the ministry of reciprocation and the Church has to stop tripping when there is seed sowing and then there is a prophetic word.

A lot of times while I am ministering, I have seen people sowing seeds in my life while I am ministering because they are sowing into the word. Nothing is wrong with that, because when you give in that atmosphere you are partnering with the Prophet, and you are sowing into the Kingdom of God for your benefit as well.

Before we go into scripture concerning giving and then a prophetic word is released, let me break down this seed giving so the Church can move from the stingy phase to the giving phase that releases the return phase.

Giving benefits the Kingdom of God and it is the love of money or the wrong attitude and relationship with money that is the root of all evil. Money answers all things according to the word, and God said all.

This is the reason why the church has to be taught, so they can stop feeling bought. Even God paid for your salvation because there is the ministry of seedtime and harvest.

We love to quote the scripture that says in Philippines 4: 13 *"But my God shall supply all your need according to his riches in glory by Christ Jesus."* However the right to quote this verse should be with the understanding of the context of scriptures that it goes with.

Let's look at verses 9-13. It says "*Those things, which ye have both learned, and received, and heard, and seen in me, do: and the God of peace shall be with you. But I rejoiced in the Lord greatly, that now at the last your care of me hath flourished again; wherein ye were also careful, but ye lacked opportunity. Not that I speak in respect of want: for I have learned, in whatsoever state I am, therewith to be content. I know both how to be abased, and I know how to abound: everywhere and in all things I am instructed both to be full and to be hungry, both to abound and to suffer need. I can do all things through Christ which strengtheneth me. Notwithstanding ye have well done, that ye did communicate with my affliction. Now ye Philippians know also, that in the beginning of the gospel, when I departed from Macedonia, no church communicated with me as concerning giving and receiving, but ye only. For even in Thessalonica ye sent once and again unto my necessity. Not because I desire a gift: but I desire fruit that may abound to your account. But I have all, and abound: I am full, having received of Epaphroditus the things which were sent from you, an odour of a sweet smell, a sacrifice acceptable, well pleasing to God. But my God shall supply all your need according to his riches in glory by Christ Jesus.*"

Paul is saying to the Philippian church that he rejoiced greatly that their care for him had flourished again; they just did not have the opportunity to get it to him. He then says it is not that I am speaking because I want your giving because I am content either way.

He then goes on to say that when he departed from Macedonia no church gave unto him concerning GIVING and RECEIVING, except for the Philippian church. Then he goes on to say that in Thessalonica they gave over and over again to him with what he needed.

Again, they gave over and over to him what he needed!

The he says something powerful, he says not that I desire a gift, but I desire fruit that may abound to your account! Then he says he has all and was full due to receiving the things they sent to him by Epaphroditus, a sacrifice acceptable and well pleasing to God!

Then he says to them that my God shall supply all your need. This was after the giving to him that would bless them. The Church has a problem looking at money as their God instead of Gods seed.

In the Kingdom of God, everything belongs to God, this is why he is Lord because Lord means owner. In the Kingdom of God you can never be broke because when you say you are broke, you are testifying that you owned the money and now what you own is gone. In the Kingdom of God we have access to the Government of Heaven, so you cannot be broke when you do not own!

Now let's look at giving and a prophetic word. In 1 Samuel 9:3-10 it says "*And the asses of Kish Saul's father were lost. And Kish said to Saul his son, Take now one of the servants with thee, and arise, go seek the asses. And he passed through mount Ephraim, and passed through the land of Shalisha, but they found them not: then they passed through the land of Shalim, and there they were not: and he passed through the land of the Benjamites, but they found them not[5] And when they were come to the land of Zuph, Saul said to his servant that was with him, Come, and let us return; lest my father leave caring for the asses, and take thought for us. And he said unto him, Behold now, there is in this city a man of God, and he is an honourable man; all that he saith cometh surely to pass: now let us go thither; peradventure he can shew us our way that we should go. Then said Saul to his servant, But, behold, if we go, what shall we bring the man? for the bread is spent in our vessels, and there is not a present to bring to the man of God: what have we? And the servant answered Saul again, and said, Behold, I have here at hand the fourth part of a shekel of silver: that will I give to the man of God, to tell us our way. (Beforetime in Israel, when a man went to enquire of God, thus he spake, Come, and let us go to the seer: for he that is now called a Prophet was beforetime called a Seer.) Then said Saul to his servant, Well said; come, let us go. So they went unto the city where the man of God was."*

Now offerings were taught by the King himself. We know this because Adam had to learn it and Cain and Abel had to learn about offerings because by faith they gave offerings and faith cometh by hearing the word of God.

Here these boys needed to know where the donkeys were, but the amazing part was that the Lord ordained to be in the Constitution of Heaven the bible, the Word of God, this story.

Notice Saul asked what we shall bring this man of God. He knew that there had to be an exchange or the ministry of reciprocation had to be enacted. He had to have been taught this obviously.

They brought money to give to him to get an answer! They said we will bring him this money so he can tell us the way!
Look at verses 19 and 20, it says *"And Samuel answered Saul, and said, I am the seer: go up before me unto the high place; for ye shall eat with me to day, and tomorrow I will let thee go, and will tell thee all that is in thine heart. And as for thine asses that were lost three days ago, set not thy mind on them; for they are found."*

So the word teaches us giving and sowing to a Prophet for release is biblical. I am not saying a Prophet should say before getting a word it will cost you. That is not what I am saying. I am showing that all through the word, there are many instances where there is a giving and then a getting.

We must understand this principle or we will get confused and hurt strictly out of ignorance.

In Article Luke Section 8 Subsections 1- 3, we see that these people were giving to Jesus out of their wealth which was their substance as he preached the gospel of the Kingdom of God.

Let's look at 1 Corinthians 9:1-14 it says, *"Am I am not an apostle? am I not free? have I not seen Jesus Christ our Lord? are not ye my work in the Lord? If I be not an apostle unto others, yet doubtless I am to you: for the seal of mine apostleship are ye in the Lord.Mine answer to them that do examine me is this, Have we not power to eat and to drink? Have we not power to lead about a sister, a wife, as well as other apostles, and as the brethren of the Lord, and Cephas? Or I only and Barnabas, have not we power to forbear working? Who goeth a warfare any time at his own charges? Who planteth a vineyard, and eateth not of the fruit thereof? or who feedeth a flock, and eateth not of the milk of the flock? Say I these things as a man? or saith not the law the same also? For it is written in the law of Moses, thou shalt not muzzle the mouth of the ox that treadeth out the corn. Doth God take care for oxen? Or saith he it altogether for our sakes? For our sakes, no doubt, this is written: that he that ploweth should plow in hope; and that he that thresheth in hope should be partaker of his hope. If we have sown unto you spiritual things, is it a great thing if we shall reap your carnal things? If others be partakers of this power over you, are not we rather? Nevertheless we have not used this power; but suffer all things, lest we should hinder the gospel of Christ. Do ye not know that they which minister about holy things live of the things of the temple? and they which wait at the altar are partakers with the altar? Even so hath the Lord ordained that they which preach the gospel should live of the gospel."*

Paul is giving an answer to those that judge, question and scrutinize him. That is the meaning of the word examine. He is asking questions in the sense of wondering what is wrong if they do this or that. Then he asks, who goes to war at his own expense. In other words you do not spend your own when going or when invited to minister.

Then he uses the scripture that talks about muzzle not the ox that treadeth out the corn, in other words if I am feeding you, don't shut my mouth to eat from you, or receive from you.

He then later asks if he is sowing spiritual, is it a big thing to reap your carnal. In other words if I am ministering to your spirit, is it such an actual crime to minister back to me of your substance?

Then he concludes that they that preach the gospel should live off the gospel.

I always recommend the understanding of itinerary ministry especially when a person is full time because if a Pastor or a person invites an itinerary ministry with an understanding, they would make sure that the one that receives the invitation should be taken care of. It does not have to be a hotel that costs an arm and a leg, but it should not be a motel filled with roaches, ants, and strange things that bite you somewhere out of nowhere.

Why? It is because they are living off the gospel as Paul mentions here.

.

So do not get discouraged when it comes to giving, this is an immature state of the Church believing that they should not sow.

If you feel led to sow into a Prophet, or Pastor, or a ministers life, obey God, no matter what others say, and watch what he will do for you!

So how do you try the spirit of a Prophet? It should be evident in their life that the work of Christ is genuinely in their lives and operation. If there works and ways uplift Christ, then that says a lot right there. A Prophet must produce the fruit of Christ in their ministry and with the Word.

Compare what they teach to the Word of God, so in essence to try the spirit is to refer to the Word of God to see if what they teach lines up with the word like the Bereans did.

Know that everything that is prophetically spoken may not always be revealed right away. There was an Ishmael before an Isaac. Do not seek Prophets for the final and only word; seek the Lord, because he is your Father and King.

In receiving a word we must understand that there can be a preceding word and a proceeding word where God has spoken one thing before and something else afterwards like with the case of Abraham for instance.

The preceding word was when God said offer Isaac, but then later in the proceeding word God said not to offer him.

So we must learn to walk in what God said before, and whatever God says to us now, and not allow the enemy to get in and cause confusion. God could be testing you and training you simultaneously.

Always pray for wisdom in applying the prophetic word received as well. Some prophetic words are conditional upon your response. If my people, then will I, in other words obey or disobey and the results are based on your reactions.

This is why when people prophesy in three days such and such, well that is a definite word that if it does not come to pass, they missed it, not you.

However we must act in faith with the word that comes forth. We must realize that if a word mentions in a few days that is prophetic terminology that does not necessarily mean in four days. That could mean months. Remember Jesus said he is coming soon thousands of years ago. So if someone prophecies that soon God is going to do this or that, don't be worrying, it will happen if God spoke it.

In other words we must understand and participate in the prophetic word received.

I remember someone prophesied to me and told me at the age of 14 that the Lord has called me to preach the gospel, but I must pray, live a fasted life, and study the word of God, and I will know when he will send me. That was a great prophetic word because it also gave instruction that I needed to follow.

I did what the Prophetess said, and then the Lord appeared to me and sent me years later. I prepared myself and participated with that prophetic word.

Responding to the prophetic however it is given must have participation. Naaman was insulted when the Prophet sent the message of instructions through someone else, but he participated with the instructions and was healed.

Can you respond like the woman who had only a little cake for herself and her son, and still give away to the Prophet? Can you follow prophetic instructions even if it seems crazy to you?

Can you really obey the Lord against all of the odds? Follow his instructions prophetically and you will always come out on top.

Ask God to bring you into the participation as well as the activation of the prophetic promise that God has spoken to you.

Do not run to every prophetic service looking for a Prophet to give you a word. Most people that do this have very short prayer lives.

God is your Father, and a Father loves to talk to his children. Get to know him more and draw closer to him, and he will speak to your heart.

Water the word you received with faith, write it down, record it if at all possible. Meditate on that prophetic word, speak that word in the atmosphere, and pray on it.

You will be surprised when you are going through and refer to that word how it lifts you up and encourages you.

A Prophets job is not to interpret what he hears, but to give what he hears. I say that because many times after a prophetic word there can be questions that you want to ask the Prophet concerning the word. They did their job, now ask the Lord.

Chapter 10

A Prophetic Word from the Lord

FOR BEHOLD THIS IS A TIME WHERE MY GLORY SHALL BE REVEALED NOT JUST IN YOUR WORSHIP LOCATIONS BUT EVEN IN THE STREETS AS I USE THE BOLD WHO ARE NOT ASHAMED OF ME AND MY WORD, THOSE THAT ARE WILLING TO GO FORTH FOR MY KINGDOM AND BE USED IN MIGHTY EXPLOITS AS I WORK MY GLORIOUS WORKS THROUGH THEM. FOR MIRACLES SHALL BE SEEN AND THE MIGHTY HAND OF THE LORD SHALL BE EXPEREINCED IN WAYS NEVER HEARD OF OR SEEN. FOR IN THESE LAST DAYS MY GLORY SHALL SHINE EVEN IN THE DARKEST PLACES OF THE WORLD AND I SHALL SPEAK PROPHETICALLY THROUGH THE LEADERS OF THE WORLD WHERE IT WOULD HAVE NEVER BEEN EXPECTED NOT EVEN BY THE CHURCH ITSELF, DO NOT TRY TO DEFEND ME FOR I CAN DEFEND MYSELF AS YOU SEE MIGHTY EXPLOITS IN THE SKIES ABOVE AND THE EARTH BELOW. FOR I AM TRADING ONE THING FOR ANOTHER, AND YOU SHALL BE A WITNESS TO THE MANIFESTIONS OF YOUR LORD AND KING, FOR THERE WILL BE LIMBS THAT WILL GROW OUT AND ASTONISH DOCTORS AND I WILL SUBMIT THE CURE FOR AIDS AND NOT EVEN BE CONCEREND ABOUT GETTING THE CREDIT

BECAUSE I KNOW WHAT I DO, AND I WILL SUBMIT THE CURE FOR CANCER AND EVEN EXPOSE THOSE THAT WOULD HOLD IT BACK. I WILL REVEAL THE HIDDEN SECRETS OF OLD AND BRING THE WHY TO THE WHAT. FOR YOU SHALL WITNESS THE REVELATION OF COUNTRIES THAT ARE HOLDING BACK MY MEN AND WOMAN OF GOD AND I WILL PUT A STOPPING IN THE MOUTHS OF THE LEADERS IN GOVERNMENT THAT WOULD TRY TO CHALLENGE ME AND USE THE MIGHTY THAT I HAVE ORDAINED TO DELIVER A NATIONAL WORD TO THEM THAT SHALL BE SEEN AND HEARD, AND SHALL SURELY COME TO PASS. FOR I AM RAISING UP THE UNKNOWN TO BE KNOWN BY MY HAND OF POWER.

FOR I SHALL EXPOSE MY GLORY THROUGH THE WILLING AND THE ANOINTED FOR I AM CHOOSING THOSE WHO THOUGHT THEY WOULD NEVER HAVE BEEN CHOSEN AND I WILL PLACE IN THE HEART OF PASTORS SUPERNATURALLY TO BRING THOSE IN AND OPEN DOORS OF CONNECTIONS TO EXPOSE MY GLORY WHERE MY GLORY WAS HELD BACK. FOR I SHALL BRING LIGHT EVEN TO THE DARK PLACES AND YOU SHALL SEE A RISING EVEN IN THE UNITED STATES OF MY GLORY SWEEPING THE STATES AND HEAR OF MY GREATNESS BEFORE MY CHURCH IS TAKEN AWAY. KNOW THAT THE DAY IS COMING WHEN I WILL PULL YOU OUT FROM THE WRATH TO COME SO WORK THE WORKS THAT I HAVE ANOINTED YOU TO WORK.

FOR I SHALL USE EVEN BABIES IN PECULIAR WAYS TO
LAY HANDS ON THE SICK TO RECOVER. I SHALL VISIT
THE HOSPITALS AND DO MIGHTY WORKS THAT
CANNOT BE EXPLAINED BY THE HOSPITAL STAFF.
SOME WILL BE ABOUT TO DIE AND HAVE FULL
RESTORATION OF HEALTH SUDDENLY TO ATTRACT
THE UNATTRACTED TO MY GLORY AND I WILL EVEN
CAUSE THE HEARTS OF THE WEAK TO BECOME
STRONG AND I WILL MEND THE BROKEN HEARTS IN
MINISTRY FOR MANY HAVE FELT THAT I HAVE
FORGOTTEN THEM BUT I HAVE NOT FORGOTTEN THEM
I WILL RESTORE MINISTRIES AND NATIONS, AND
PEOPLE LIKE NEVER BEFORE.

FOR I AM THE LORD THAT OWNS THE EARTH AND I
WILL CAUSE A SHAKENING IN THE EARTH FOR
ATTENTION TO MY THRONE FOR I AM THE ULTIMATE
JUDGE FOR I SEE THE HAPPENINGS IN EARTH AND THE
SINFUL WAYS OF MANKIND AND I WILL REDEEM WHO
I WILL REDEEM AND I WILL PUNISH WHO I WILL
PUNISH AND I WILL BUILD UP WHERE I DESIRE FOR MY
GLORY AND PLEASEURE. ADD NO WORDS TO THE
THINGS I SAY AND TAKE AWAY NO WORDS FROM THE
THINGS IS SAY KNOW THAT THIS IS A TIME FOR
REVELATION IN THE BODY OF CHIRST LIKE NEVER
BEFORE AND I SHALL REVEAL TRUTHS TO THE
HUNGRY SEEKERS AND I SHALL FILL THE HUNGER OF
THE CHURCH AND I WILL USE YOU TO IGNITE JOY IN
OTHERS AND I SHALL USE YOU THAT WERE IN THE
BACK UNNOTICED AND NOT ACCEPETED EVEN TO
YOU THAT TRY TO BUILD MINISTRIES FOR YOUR GLORY
I SHALL BRING YOU TO YOUR KNEES IN REPENTANCE
AND CONFESSION AND CAUSE YOU TO BE HUMBLE IN
MY SIGHT AND THE SIGHT OF MEN

FOR I SHALL COAT MY CHILDREN FAR AND NEAR WITH FAVOR IN PECULIAR WAYS AND CAUSE CONNECTIONS WITH MANY WHERE OTHERS COULD NOT CONNECT, FOR THERE SHALL BE MANY MORE DISEASES COMING TO MANKIND AND SOME WILL BE PUT TOGETHER BY MAN EVEN IN THE SECRET PLACE AND IT WOULD BE AS THOUGH IT CAME FROM THE SWIMMING CREATURES FOR BEHOLD I REVEAL THE SECRETS OF MY HEART TO YOU EVEN AS YOU SEE MY WORDS AND I WILL VISIT YOU WHEN YOU LEAST EXPECT AND REVEAL MANY TRUTHS TO YOU I SHALL EVEN CAUSE A STUNT IN NEGATIVITY THAT ATTEMPTS TO GROW IN GROUPS THAT ATTACK WITH TERRORISM AND FEAR FOR I AM BULIDING A GROUP THAT WILL COME AGAINST THE THINGS OF THE ENEMY BUT BE IT KNOWN THAT HARD TIMES SHALL HIT THE EARTH LIKE NEVER BEFORE EVEN BEFORE THE CHURCH IS TAKEN OUT BUT BE OF GOOD CHEER FOR I HAVE ALREADY GIVEN YOU THE VICTORY!

This word from the Lord flowed straight out of my spirit and so I placed it in this book and literally typed as it came and flowed. I make no apologies for grammatical errors for I dare not touch and try to make proper the flow of the Spirit based on commas, etc.

May the Kingdom Blessings of Heaven be with you as he prophetically utters his word, will, purpose, desire, design, and wisdom into your hearts!